Alaska, U.S.A.

Also by Herb Hilscher

ALASKA NOW
(1948)

Alaska, U.S.A.

By Herb and Miriam Hilscher

With Photographs

Little, Brown and Company
Boston · Toronto

LIBRARY OF CONGRESS CATALOG CARD NO. 59–14539

FOURTH PRINTING

*Published simultaneously in Canada
by Little, Brown & Company (Canada) Limited*

PRINTED IN THE UNITED STATES OF AMERICA

To those who pioneered Alaska . . .

To those who crusaded for statehood . . .

To those who are now working to make

    the state of Alaska a vital force

    in our American way of life . . .

This book is affectionately dedicated

Authors' Note

EDNA FERBER sat in a semicircle of twenty young Alaskans in the king-sized living room of Bob and Evangeline Atwood's home in Anchorage. Four-foot birch logs crackled warmly in the stone fireplace and gave forth a glow that danced highlights in the eyes of those who had come to meet the famous author.

As keen an observer as exists in the literary world today, Miss Ferber declared earnestly, "I have never felt anywhere the drive, the urge, the idealism, the youth and the compelling spirit of achievement that I have in Alaska. It thrills me. I feel it all over the Northland. It's like the twentieth-century fire in men's souls that was present three generations ago in the settling of the West."

Miss Ferber was gathering material for her *Ice Palace,* a novel that helped to plead eloquently the cause of statehood for Alaska.

She looked around the circle at the young lawyers, engineers, legislators, artists, writers and businessmen — men and women who were helping to shape the destiny of Alaska. Their average age was under forty.

Miss Ferber questioned each person. She wanted to know exactly why these people had come to Alaska.

Their backgrounds were different, their birthplaces were

varied. But she discovered their reasons for coming to Alaska — and staying — were strikingly similar.

They were here because Alaska is a land where youth and ambition, ideals and zest for achievement, warm red blood and bold enterprise set the pace for living. The reward for effort is the achievement of goals new in the scheme of things Alaskan — new in the consciousness of a better society.

None of these young people would think of returning to the old 48 states. Alaska is their home. Their hearts, their roots and their destinies are here.

It is to present a picture of this compelling force and drive, this desire to make Number 49 one of the most dynamic states in the Union, that this book has been written.

It attempts to let you feel the heartbeat and the pulse of the vast awakening Northland, and to give you an accurate look at its opportunities — as well as its discouragements, hardships and pitfalls.

Many Alaskans helped to mold this book. By their deeds and accomplishments for the advancement of our Alaskan way of life, they have contributed to these pages and to the destiny of Alaska.

The 49th state is growing at an amazing pace. Astonishing developments are taking place. Tremendous projects for the future are now in the making.

This book is a portrait of the new state — Alaska, U.S.A.

Contents

(Photographs between pages 116 and 117)

STATE OF ALASKA

—— Paved Roads   -------- Improved Roads

• Population under 1,000   ● 1,000–5,000   ⊙ 5,000–10,000   ⊕ 10,000–25,000

⊛ Capital city   0 40 80 120 160 200   and up

SCALE OF MILES

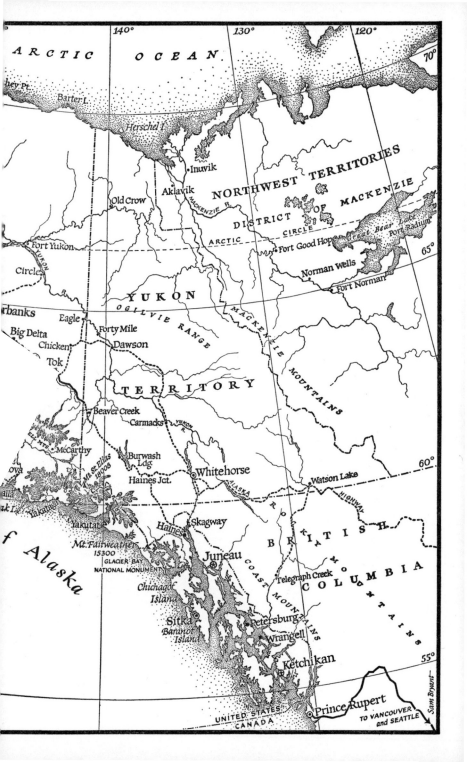

Alaska, U.S.A.

1

Alaskan History in a Capsule

ONE OF THE FIRST AMERICANS TO VISIT ALASKA
was so taken with what he saw that he spent the rest of his
life trying to get back to the Northland.

He never made it. But his almost fanatical enthusiasm for
the "Great Land" and his fabulous tales of the wealth it
possessed influenced other Americans to expand their horizons westward and to enlarge the shape and dimensions of
the United States.

This young adventurer was John Ledyard, a divinity stu-
dent who left Dartmouth College because of an "uncon-
trollable desire to see the world," and wound up on Captain
Cook's flagship on the third voyage of discovery around the
world.

This history-making voyage took the young American
northward along the coast of what is now Oregon, Washington, British Columbia and Alaska — almost to Point Barrow. In that year, 1778, the Pacific Northwest was an un-
charted wilderness, and the lofty snow-clad peaks and
mile-wide glaciers had been seen by few.

Ledyard fell in love with the country and was utterly
enthralled by its potential. For only a few beads and trinkets

the crew bought beautiful otter and beaver pelts which they later sold in Canton for a hundred dollars each!

When he returned to America four years later, Ledyard tried desperately to get backing for a ship to enter the lucrative Alaska-Canton fur trade. His tales of the profits to be made were so fantastic that shipowners simply would not believe him.

Undismayed, he went to Paris, where he met United States Minister Thomas Jefferson, and here started a friendship which turned out to be prophetic for the United States. Ledyard confided to Jefferson his plan to get a ship, sail to the west coast and Alaska, fill the ship with furs, and send it off to Canton. Ledyard himself would walk home eastward across the Great Land and the unexplored American continent in hopes of finding a shorter route to his fur supply. Perhaps the vast country could be added to the new American nation.

Jefferson was so impressed with Ledyard's vision — and so enamored with his idea of exploring North America — that he was instrumental in helping the young man get a ship financed and outfitted in London.

The ship never sailed. It was said that the British Hudson's Bay Company, which had a chartered fur monopoly in the New World, wanted no competition and put pressure on the Crown to seize the vessel.

An effort of Ledyard's to get to Alaska by way of Siberia also failed. After hitchhiking five thousand miles across Europe and Asia, with promise of passage on a ship from Siberia to Alaska, "Walking John" was arrested in Yakutsk by Cossacks, brought back to Europe and dumped over the Polish border. He had been charged vaguely with being a French spy, but rumor had it that Siberian merchants wanted no one to see their wanton exploitation of the Great Land.

Ledyard, broke and disheartened, accepted the leadership of a scientific expedition in Africa. He died in Cairo at the age of thirty-eight, still hoping to get back to Alaska.

Thirteen years later, Thomas Jefferson became President of the United States. Remembering John Ledyard's tales of the great wealth of the Pacific, he sent his personal secretary, Meriwether Lewis, and Captain William Clark on the first overland expedition to the Pacific coast. As a result of this trek, the American press claimed every bit of terrain from California north to Alaska for the United States.

John Ledyard's dream lived on. Yankee shipowners, whom he had tried to interest in fur trading in Alaska a quarter of a century before, now dominated the fur trade of the north Pacific coast. Later San Francisco merchants made inroads on the Russian domain. Russia's hold on the Great Land began to get shaky.

But we must backtrack a bit. Back to the first white man in Alaska's life. Back to a sixty-year-old Dane, fatally ill of scurvy, who never set foot on Alaska's shores, who anchored but a few hours in the shadow of her towering mountains, yet, through the courtesy of historians, is credited with discovering the Great Land.

Vitus Bering, a Danish sea captain working for the Russian Navy, was the commander of a two-ship expedition sent out by Peter the Great to claim the unknown land for the Czar.

The ships were separated in a storm, and the *St. Paul*, captained by Alexei Chirikof, limped back to Kamchatka three months later with every man suffering from scurvy. Seven had died from the disease.

Bering's ship, the *St. Peter*, dropped anchor off Kayak

Island, near the mouth of the Copper River, on July 16, 1741, and thus Alaskan history starts with Bering's name.

Bering, suffering from scurvy, sent sailors ashore for fresh water. Hardly had they filled half the barrels and brought them aboard when the captain-commander decided to up the anchor and head for home. Seventy-eight men were crowded aboard a ship only eighty feet long and twenty feet wide, and many of them were learned scholars rather than experienced sailors. The *St. Peter* battled full gales in the North Pacific and thirty-one of the crew died of scurvy.

The ship was almost a derelict when she put into what is now Bering Island in the Komandorskies, and for a while the crew thought they had landed back in Siberia. Here Bering died of scurvy, and was buried in the sand under a simple Orthodox cross.

And now the quirk of fate, the smirk of history. For food and clothing during that miserable winter, the men hunted the sea otter and the fur seal. When the survivors reached Kamchatka the following year they brought with them an astounding collection of furs worth $100,000. These pelts set Siberia on fire, and every merchant, nobleman, trader and freebooter who could buy, borrow or build a craft pushed off for the Komandorskies, the Aleutians, and finally the mainland of Alaska.

For crews, the jails of Siberia were swept clean, and serfs and peasants were shanghaied aboard.

Principle, honesty and fair dealing with the simple Aleuts played no part in the frenzy for furs. The Aleut women were captured en masse. Whole villages of Aleut men were enslaved to hunt the sea otter. What matter if a thousand men died in storms at sea! Another thousand would be rounded up at gun point. Twenty-five thousand Aleuts were living peacefully along the Chain when the Russian freebooters arrived. Five decades later the population had been decimated to a pitiful two thousand.

But eventually tales of this human carnage and the destruction of the fur-bearing animals reached the ears of the Czar. He ordered an end to freebooting and chartered one company — the Russian-American Company — to be responsible for all trade, commerce, government, education, and the spread of the Orthodox faith in Alaska.

Alexander Baranof, a successful Irkutsk merchant, was hired as manager of the company, and Alaska was introduced to the pleasures and growing pains of the white man's civilization. Baranof ruled as a benevolent despot, first at Kodiak and then from his castle at Sitka, entertaining lavishly with all the elegance befitting his importance.

Isolated from his homeland and the companionship and counsel of his equals, Baranof was deluged with problems. One he could not control was the encroachment of Yankee ships, British ships, and vessels of other nations which raided his shores, trading rot-gut rum for furs. What these buccaneers could not get with trinkets and calico, they often took by force and gunpowder.

In the glory days of Sitka, Alexander Baranof built his niche in history. But greatness breeds jealousy, and the covetous brass of the Imperial Navy finally succeeded in deposing the great man. Baranof left Alaska broken in spirit and health, and destiny decreed that he should never return to his homeland. He was buried at sea in the Indian Ocean.

From then on, Russia's fortunes and her foothold in Alaska crumbled rapidly.

Overtures were made to sell Alaska to the United States

before the Civil War. The time was not ripe. But at the close of the War Between the States, with William Henry Seward as Secretary of State, events moved to a quick climax.

Seward was an expansionist. He envisioned the United States as encompassing everything from the seals of the frozen Arctic to the bananas of Panama. He believed the capital of the expanding nation eventually should be in salubrious Mexico City!

Seward reasoned, "Why shouldn't the United States buy Alaska? It's a bargain at less than two cents per acre."

The deal was signed at 4:00 A.M. on March 30, 1867, with the flourishes of William Henry Seward, buyer, and Baron Edouard de Stoeckl, the Russian Minister, seller. The transfer of Alaska to the United States took place at Sitka on the afternoon of Friday, October 18, 1867, and the war-weary nation became a king-sized landowner of the Western world.

The House of Representatives, however was not so hot for Seward's Ice Box, and took its merry sweet time providing the cash for the Secretary's early-morning real estate deal. It was not until nine months later that Russia finally received her $7,200,000 payment from the United States.

Sitka was host to William Henry Seward on his triumphant tour around the world a year later. Here the former Secretary, a flowery orator, made the first pitch for statehood for Alaska. He predicted, "Nor do I doubt that the political society to be constituted here, first as a territory and ultimately as a state or many states, will prove a worthy constituency of the Republic."

Now that Alaska was American soil, which department of the federal government would be saddled with its administration? Nobody wanted the job. But because the Army had put on a show of uniforms and muskets when the Double Eagle came down at Sitka, and a battalion was still stationed there, the Army got the business.

With nothing to keep the troops occupied, law and order slipped. With time on their hands, and barrels of molasses for making hooch, the situation soon spiraled into "hooch-klooch-smooch." Some squaws were more than agreeable, but their husbands reacted violently. Finally faraway Washington heard of the bacchanalian festival. The Army sailed south.

Now the moccasin was on the other foot. The Indians had been just so much expendable flesh to the early Russian fur seekers. They had been harshly treated by other early-day buccaneers. Then the hard-drinking American soldiers had spent a total of almost ten years lightening the complexion of the younger native generation.

All the grievances, all the pent-up hate of almost a hundred years could be avenged in one first-class massacre. The Collector of Customs, who was the sole government agent left in Alaska, tried frantically to get a revenue cutter from Puget Sound, finally wrote Washington pleading for protection. The Secretary of the Treasury recommended only that the Customs District of Alaska be abolished.

In desperation, the citizens of Sitka petitioned the British at Victoria for help. They responded with dignity — and a frigate.

For the first time in months Sitkans slept soundly. The native drums stopped beating and the war paint came off. Uncle Sam was shamed into action, and in mid-June the U.S.S. *Jamestown* arrived in Sitka harbor. From then on, for the next two decades, there was a United States vessel in Alaskan waters.

From the date of purchase until it achieved statehood ninety-two years later, Alaska's history was directed and influenced in large measure by wealthy Outside interests.

Certain California companies had been active in promoting the purchase of Alaska. They saw the opportunity of succeeding to the empire of the Russian-American Company and gaining a virtual monopoly of trade in the Northland. Hutchinson, Kohl & Company of San Francisco was represented in Sitka the day the Russian flag came down. From Prince Maksoutoff, the last Russian overseer, they purchased the assets of the Russian-American Company.

Two years later the Alaska Commercial Company of San Francisco bought out Hutchinson, Kohl & Company, and obtained from Congress an exclusive twenty-year franchise to the fur seal rookeries of the Pribilof Islands.

Thus started the second chapter of exploitation of Alaska's wealth — the large American concerns which helped themselves not only to Alaska's furs but to her gold and fish as well.

These monopolies wanted only one thing — profits. Big profits. They scorned any responsibility for building up the country. The lobbyists they kept in Washington to "advise" Congress on Alaska were there for one purpose only: to keep Alaska without population and government.

Alaska's handful of residents was no match for the influence of the monopolies, and for a long time their protestations were of no avail.

But there was a deep, humane force at work in the Territory which slowly but surely made itself felt in official Washington. To the selfless, dedicated missionaries who carried the word of God to the natives and whites in the Northland goes credit for the still small voice that made

Congressmen and Senators stop and listen to the needs of Alaska.

The case for the neglected Territory was summarized by crusader Rev. Sheldon Jackson in the last paragraph of his widely read book *Alaska:* "Let the Congress of the United States provide Alaska with a government and a system of common and industrial schools. Let the Christian churches hasten to send in missionaries, and a brighter day will dawn upon that long and sadly neglected portion of our common country."

Sheldon Jackson was a tireless advocate of Alaska. He wrote letters endlessly to the editors of important newspapers. He spoke to church conventions on the wealth and opportunity of the Territory. He called on every denomination — Protestants and Catholics alike — to send missionaries to Alaska. He solicited funds for schools and churches for the Northland. Through the congregations of the United States he awakened the American conscience to the shameless neglect by Congress.

"Russia gave them [the natives] government, schools and the Greek religion, but when the country passed from their possession they withdrew their rulers, priests and teachers, while the United States did not send any others to take their place. Alaska, today, has neither courts, rulers, ministers, nor teachers. The only thing the United States has done for them has been to introduce whiskey." With this stinging rebuke Jackson indicted the United States government.

The Organic Act of 1884 was an act of conscience. The first enactment of any type of government for Alaska, it provided for a governor, a district court, an attorney, a clerk, four marshals and four commissioners. The laws of Oregon (for no good reason) were made to apply to Alaska. Marriage

was now legal, and property could be recorded and transferred. The importation of whiskey was forbidden.

Each Christian mission was granted 640 acres of land, and
the munificent sum of $25,000 was appropriated for schools.
Sheldon Jackson was named commissioner of education.

But, thanks to the lobby, the Organic Act had been so
badly drafted that it was virtually a nullity, and it plagued
Alaska until the turn of the century. Homesteading provisions
were stricken from the original bill.

Along with the missionaries and the representatives of
Outside interests, explorers, government surveyors and other
adventurous souls began to discover Alaska. In 1879 John
Muir, the naturalist, made a trip to the Panhandle to study
glaciers. Muir also knew a good deal about geology, and
he expressed the belief that there were high-grade gold
deposits not far from Glacier Bay.

Two Sitka miners took a chance on Muir's geology and the
next year camped at the site of the present town of Juneau.
They found rich placer ground. A stampede pulled miners
out of the Cassiar, the Stikine, the Fraser country — even
from the gold creeks of Oregon and California. Juneau began
to boom, and in 1883 more than $300,000 in nuggets and dust
were mined. High-grade lode was found across the channel,
and the Treadwell mine became a bonanza that attracted
the attention of the mining world.

For the next quarter-century gold was the magnet that
drew population northward. Placer gold was found in the
interior in 1886, and a trickle of men went into the Fortymile
country — to Franklin Gulch and Chicken Creek.

In 1894 Circle City blossomed on the banks of the Yukon
when gold was found in the streams nearby. A thousand men
were now in the Yukon Valley and each year more ad-

venturers joined the quest for gold in the Land of the Midnight Sun.

Then came the Klondike.

August 17, 1896, started out like any other day for the prospectors on Bonanza Creek. Kate, the faithful squaw of George Carmack, had fried some fish for her white man and for her brothers Skookum Jim and Tagish Charlie. She took her skillet down to the creek, filled it with dirt and water, and cleaned it prospector fashion. As she washed it out, half a dozen colors sparkled in the bottom. She looked again. Then, shouting "George! George! We've got it!" she rushed up the bank to the waiting men.

Exactly eleven months later the S.S. *Portland* docked in Seattle with the cleanup from the Klondike. The newspapers of the world screamed the "Ton of Gold" story which has become the Klondike legend.

Thus started one of the most spectacular gold rushes in history — the Klondike stampede. Every person — male or female — who could raise the price of the fare and grubstake pushed off for the Northland.

At the turn of the century gold was discovered on the Seward Peninsula by Swedish Covenant missionaries, and there was a rush to Nome. Felix Pedro found colors in the Tanana Valley, and the mining town of Fairbanks mushroomed on the banks of the Chena River.

Prospectors fanned out over the vast Interior and dug potholes on virtually every stream. Trails crisscrossed the Territory, roadhouses blossomed, cabins were built, villages grew like Topsy and ornate stern-wheelers puffed and chuffed up and down the Yukon and Tanana rivers.

Preachers and priests were passengers on the same steamers that brought the dance-hall girls and cargoes of whiskey to Alaska. It was often said that, if all the whiskey consumed in Alaska during the stampede days had been poured into one enormous lake, it would have been enough to float the whole Territory out into the middle of the Pacific Ocean.

Churches in the States prayed and paid for the work of the Lord in the Northland, and rang the steeple bells for Christian life in Alaska. Clergy were assigned to various communities, and congregations were soon assembled.

After Soapy Smith made lawlessness a profession in Skagway in 1898, Congress again wrestled with the Alaska problem, and a criminal code was passed for the Northland.

In 1906 Alaska was given a voteless delegate to sit in the United States House of Representatives, but it took another six years of tireless effort to achieve official territorial status. Congress granted Alaska a legislature with limited powers: every act it passed was subject to veto by Congress, and this applied right up to statehood.

Alaska's first territorial legislature was elected in 1912 on a nonpartisan basis, and its first official act gave women the right to vote — seven years before the Nineteenth Amendment was adopted by the United States.

During the first decade of the twentieth century, big Outside mining interests entered Alaska. The rich Kennecott copper mine 190 miles inland from Cordova became a stellar producer, and a railroad was built to bring the ore to the seacoast at Cordova.

This was also the period of salmon cannery expansion, and it was not unusual for a million-dollar Alaskan cannery to pay for itself in a season or two.

It took an era of political scandal in Washington, D. C.,

to end the freebooting days of uncontrolled exploitation in Alaska. The people of the United States and Congress were shocked at the way the robber barons had cut clean the forests of the Midwest, at the great land scandals of the Western railroads, at the destruction of the vast stands of timber in Oregon and Washington. A great wave of conservation swept the country and engulfed Alaska. As a result of this, coal and oil leases were canceled, and all of Southeastern Alaska and part of Southcentral Alaska were established as national forests. Alaska's expansion came to a standstill.

In 1913 President Wilson took an interest in the Territory's ills and sponsored a railroad from the seaport town of Seward to Fairbanks in the Interior. Construction of the Alaska Railroad was begun in 1915, using the well-worn equipment and rolling stock that built the Panama Canal. The town of Anchorage came into being as headquarters for the railroad.

But by the time the government-owned railway was completed in 1923, Alaska was well into a slump. The best gold-mining ground had been skimmed. Alaska's population had declined. Businesses, buildings and inventories in many a town could be bought for a fraction of their value.

Then, slowly, big-time mining began to stage a comeback in the Interior. The United States Smelting, Refining and Mining Company of Boston was sold on operations in the Territory by a young mining engineer named Norman Stines. Stines reasoned that the Alaska Railroad could slash shipping costs to a fraction, electric power from the vast coalfield nearby could run mammoth dredges, and modern mining methods could make marginal land pay off handsomely. Later Stines interested the same company in lucrative gold-dredging operations at Nome.

When President Franklin Delano Roosevelt increased the price of gold from $20.67 to $35 an ounce, gold production rose from $9,700,000 in 1933 to $26,000,000 in 1940. Forty-eight dredges were operating throughout the Territory, and scores of hydraulic giants and noisy caterpillars scoured placer creeks.

The publicity which flooded the nation when 209 families from the Middle West were sent to the Matanuska Valley to farm in 1935 again put Alaska on the front page. To this day, the Matanuska Valley is one of the most widely known recognition features of Alaska.

Roosevelt's regime also brought federal projects and federal grants to the Territory — aids to airports and aviation, aids to agriculture, a public works program, and the extension of the Federal Housing Administration to Alaska. A hotel was built by the Department of the Interior in McKinley National Park to encourage tourist travel to the Northland.

Plans for a rustic chalet-type hotel that would give the Alaskan atmosphere were put in the ashcan by Potomac architects, and, in the words of the late Colonel Otto F. Ohlson, then general manager of the Alaska Railroad, "We got a flat-roofed, elongated monstrosity, like a boxcar, that the Navajos would have burned had it been on their reservation. But we were so damn glad to get *anything* that we said, 'It's wonderful!'"

Another turning point in Alaska's history occurred in 1939 when Roosevelt appointed Dr. Ernest Gruening, Director of the Division of Territories and Island Possessions, to be Governor of Alaska. Gruening, more than any one person, was destined to guide Alaska out of adolescent thinking. He taught Alaskans the fine points of politics, economics and social progress for the Territory.

Gruening's appointment was the beginning of the bitter decline of the absentee rulers of Alaska. Gruening was a graduate of the rough and tumble school of politics, and he gave as well as he took. He battled the skillful Outside interests, weakened their influence over the territorial legislature, then carried Alaska's crusade to the United States Congress.

In April, 1940, Washington, D. C., discovered the strategic importance of Alaska, and since that date close to three billion dollars have been invested in the Northland in all phases of defense of the Western world.

Thousands of young men stationed in Alaska during the war became salesmen for the Territory. Many of them returned to Alaska to homestead, to work, or to go into business for themselves. Alaska became publicized as America's last great frontier. "Go North, young man" thrilled young people as "Go West, young man" did an earlier generation.

Alaska's population doubled in less than twenty years, and the zeal for full equality with citizens living in the States became a burning passion, a flaming goal to be achieved. Most of Alaska's residents came from the States, and they protested being demoted to second-class citizenship — to colonial status.

Because Alaska's government was subject to the whims of the Department of the Interior, big money would not invest in the Northland. The economy of the Territory was being bolstered primarily by defense appropriations which were increased every time the Kremlin got dyspepsia.

When Congress granted statehood to Alaska in 1958, interest in the new 49th state became overpowering. Alaska was anew the promised land.

The achievement of statehood is still so new that Alaskans are overwhelmed by its reality. The 49th state is now in the honeymoon stage of its relationship with the nation. Everyone wishes Alaska success, and expects big things of it.

Even while Alaskans welcome their new-found freedom, many long-time Sourdoughs glance back nostalgically at the rugged romantic era of the Northland which is no more. The riverboats which plied the Yukon and Tanana rivers are gone. The winter stages and the old-style roadhouses no longer exist. Only one dog team still carries the United States mail to a remote Eskimo village.

Except for summer cruise ships, and Canadian service to a few Southeastern ports, there is no longer any passenger steamship service to Alaska. The airplane and the Alaska Highway have taken over, bringing Alaska closer to the rest of the United States — and Alaskans into a closer camaraderie with one another. Progress has engulfed the Northland.

The new citizens of Alaska realize that they must think big to accomplish big things. Already there is a rising stream of population northward. Risk capital is arriving on every plane. Startling development projects are coming off the drafting boards.

But more important than any of these things is the feeling in the hearts of Alaskans that the responsibility for making this a great new state is now theirs alone. They are willing to accept this responsibility.

Alaska has come of age!

Book One

2

Three Minutes on Alaska

A MILLION PEOPLE HAVE THE ALASKA FEVER —
bad. They just can't wait to head north to the 49th state. The
wide open spaces. The gold nuggets waiting for their shovel.
The rainbow trout two feet long. The fertile homesteads that
will make them landed barons — the easy way.

To these twentieth-century pioneers, statehood has con-
jured up visions of opportunities unlimited and jobs for
everyone. To them Alaska is the promised land — the new
Utopia.

The rush north is growing day by day. We Alaskans are
powerless to stop it. We wouldn't if we could. But we plead
that these good people know what they are getting into
before they burn their bridges behind them and, on arrival
here, expect the bounty of nature and the big heart of the
new state to bless them with abundance, wealth and happi-
ness.

Opportunities are unlimited in Alaska — for the right
persons. Many young couples have hit the jackpot up here
much sooner than they would have in the Lower 48. But they
have hit it the old-fashioned way: by hard work, long hours,
personal sacrifice and a special brand of stick-to-it-iveness.

Not by a forty-hour week, jobless insurance and unemployment compensation.

Increasingly we hear Cheechakos say, "If only we had known more about Alaska before we came north. If only we had had an honest picture of the hardships and discouragements of life up here. If only we could have weighed the bad with the good, then we would have been better prepared for Alaska."

Due to misinformation, gilding the lily, exuberant journalism and doubtful reporting, thousands and thousands will come north who should never leave their homes Outside. Alaska will be damned, cursed and vilified by those who find conditions in the Northland not to their liking and return home to declare the new state to be a fraud and its citizens scoundrels.

Out of our years of experience in Alaska, we Sourdoughs have a few suggestions we'd like to pass on to would-be Alaskans before they quit their jobs in the other states and start north.

(1) Before taking off for Alaska, have a round-trip ticket in your pocket and at least $500 in travelers' checks to cover expenses while you give the 49th state the once-over-lightly. After seeing Alaska you may say, "I don't want any part of it."

(2) But if you like Alaska, see all of it before you decide where you want to settle, to put down roots. Let the wife do a lot of the deciding on where in the new state you will make your home.

(3) If you are planning on getting a job in Alaska, please read the chapter "Want a Job in Alaska?" before you start north. It can save you a lot of heartaches. Don't come north with the idea of making a pile in a year or two and then

getting the hell out of the country. Those days are gone forever!

(4) If you are planning on driving to Alaska, start with a good car. You are inviting nothing but trouble if you load up an old jalopy and a trailer that is past its prime.

(5) If you decide to settle in Alaska, come properly prepared. A rock-bottom minimum to tide you over until you get your stride is $5000. Living costs are from 19 to 55 per cent higher than in the Northwest, and going into business up here usually takes more capital than you had planned.

We Alaskans expect that within twenty years there will be a million citizens living in the new state where today there are but 225,000. And as population increases and civilization advances life will become easier in the Northland. In the meantime, in spite of its magnetic power, Alaska is still The Last Frontier.

3

An Awful Lot of Real Estate

ALASKA IS AN AWFUL LOT OF REAL ESTATE. IT IS the biggest land deal Uncle Sam ever stumbled into, and he is reaping a bumper fortune from his investment.

Alaska is so large it has to be cut up into chunks to be talked about and digested. If you were to pick up the 49th state, and place it dripping wet on top of the continental United States, Ketchikan would dip into the Atlantic Ocean below Charleston, Point Barrow would cross the Canadian border above Duluth, and Attu would extend into the Pacific Ocean off the coast of California near Santa Barbara.

So vast a domain needs a husky backbone, and the cordillera of coastal mountains and the Rockies combine into a stupendous range that forms a long-sweeping arc across the Great Land. It starts in the Panhandle, curves through the heart of the state, and continues on to the end of the Aleutian Chain. From this backbone soar the tallest mountains in North America. Mammoth glaciers flow down its valleys, and age-old volcanoes still smolder, steam and explode.

Geography is a matter of viewpoint, and your impressions of Alaska — its shape, its size, its scenery and its character — depend upon how you travel to the new state.

If you drive to Alaska, you approach the Northland over the endless, rolling plains of northern Canada. Once you cross the border you traverse an unbelievable expanse of plateau land, with craggy ranges and snow-capped peaks far off in the distance.

If you fly north from Seattle, mountains stretch endlessly below you. There is scarcely a square foot of flat land in sight.

If you come to the 49th state on a cruise ship, you wind continuously through sun-splashed fiords, with green, picture-book mountains rising sheer on all sides.

Alaska is all of these things — and more. It is more than twice the size of Texas — and has less population than Wyoming. You can fly for miles and miles over the new state and not see a cabin, a road, or a fishing boat. When you drive through Alaska, civilization does not stretch from one community to another. It exists in small patches. It ceases a few miles out of town, and, except for an occasional roadhouse or eating spot, doesn't appear again until you reach the next wide place in the road.

You simply cannot generalize about the new state any more than you can describe the Old 48 in one paragraph. Nature and man have divided Alaska into four geographical, economic and political units: Southeastern Alaska, South-central Alaska, Central Alaska and Northwestern Alaska.

Southeastern Alaska, or the Panhandle, is about the size of Indiana. It got its name because it looks like a panhandle — and because, in the decades before statehood, the experienced politicians of this once all-influential section controlled and maneuvered the rest of the Northland as a chef manipulates a huge skillet.

Southeastern Alaska is the realm of canned salmon, fresh

and frozen fish, pulp, timber and tourists. It is a mass of islands and mountainous coastline extending northward for five hundred miles. Sitka, the old Russian capital, and Juneau, the present seat of government, are both here.

The countless islands of Southeastern Alaska are densely mantled in vertical green forests which, for centuries, have grown, ripened and fallen — a total economic waste. But this voiceless wilderness of usable timber could supply endlessly more than one-third of the newsprint needs of the nation if and when it is scientifically managed and harvested.

Southcentral Alaska, which is about the size of Oregon, includes the land from the Gulf of Alaska north to the Alaska Range, and westerly to the end of the Aleutian Chain. In this area is Alaska's biggest city, the highest mountain on the continent, and here commercial petroleum was discovered in 1957. Here, too, are the famous Matanuska Valley, the headquarters for the Alaska Defense Command, and much of Alaska's wealth in salmon and other sea products.

The Central district of Alaska covers the vast Interior — an area as large as Texas. It stretches from the Alaska Range northward along the Canadian border to the Arctic Ocean, westward to the mid-Arctic, then meanders southwesterly in a huge, wide sweep all the way to Bristol Bay and the Bering Sea.

The one metropolitan community in this entire district is Fairbanks, and around this city are air installations to protect us from sudden attack over the Pole. Here are potential farming and livestock areas. Here are millions of acres of land which are under federal lease for oil and gas exploration.

Outside of Fairbanks, the vast Interior is a virgin frontier. There are less than a hundred villages, trading posts and pinpoints on the map in this entire empire with a post office where you can buy a postage stamp or mail a letter.

The fourth district is Northwestern Alaska. It is the size of Iowa, Arkansas and Missouri combined. For untold generations it has been the undisputed domain of the Eskimos who lived on walrus and seal and polar bear. But the mystery of the Arctic slopes has disappeared like a mist before the invasion of the airplane and the DEW Line, the radar defense network of the North. These changes in the economy of the Arctic are transplanting the majority of the ten thousand Eskimos from a blubber and seal oil civilization to the doubtful eminence of living with steaks, bubble gum and airborne corn on the cob.

In this part of Alaska, only two and one-half miles of water separate Russian Big Diomede Island from Alaska's Little Diomede Island. And from Cape Prince of Wales, in Alaska, to East Cape, Siberia, it is but fifty-four miles. As you fly along the coast of the Seward Peninsula, looking across the International Dateline from Sunday into Monday, the mainland of Siberia looms on the horizon like a distant, ominous mass.

What lies within the boundaries of the four districts of Alaska? Some of the greatest resources of our world, still unexplored, climate just as varied as the terrain, towns and hamlets unique to the Alaskan pattern and others just like Main Street, U. S. A.

Geographically speaking, the first city of Alaska is Ketchikan, which is closer to Seattle than it is to Point Barrow. As a tourist you may see only the heart of the downtown shopping area, but Ketchikan boasts tall apartments, modern homes, a $55,000,000 pulp mill, and the title of All-America City.

Totem poles stand guard here and there in Ketchikan, and

you will take home hand-carved miniatures as mementos of your trip to Alaska. Close by the first city is the native village of Saxman, with its tall collection of photogenic and legendary totems, standing as mute sentinels of the culture of a bygone era.

Ketchikan is famed for its summer-long fishing derby. If you have not matched wits with a forty-pound king salmon on light tackle, and battled him to a finish alongside your skiff, you just haven't lived! It's worth the trip to Alaska just to experience this thrill.

Although it rains 150 inches per year (that's twelve and a half feet) in Ketchikan, it doesn't dampen the spirit of the residents, and it keeps the forests green. You can be wet in more ways than one in this friendly community. Here many a tourist gets his first introduction to hospitality by the bottle or by the drink so prevalent in Alaska.

In Ketchikan, too, you will meet the typical Alaskan spirit of independence. Here is a delightful restaurant with excellent food, and the place is jammed with customers. The man and wife who run it work furiously for several months. Then they say "To hell with it!" They lock the front door, hang out a sign saying "WILL BE BACK IN TWO OR THREE WEEKS," and take off for all points of the compass.

Unless you are on a cruise ship, the only way you can travel from town to town in the Panhandle land of islands and ocean is by airplane. Except for limited Canadian steamship service, there are no passenger ships on the Alaskan run. So you climb aboard an eight-passenger Grumman Goose that sits in the water, fasten your seat belt, and, with a mighty roar, take off like a powered surfboard.

En route to Wrangell you fly over small fishing boats trolling for salmon, and seiners circling schools of fish with huge purse nets. Often you see deer on the peaks as your plane scoots by.

Wrangell is one of the oldest towns in Alaska. It entered the pages of our history as a native community. Then came the Russians who built Fort St. Dionysius to resist the encroachments of the Hudson's Bay Company. Here one of the earliest Christian missions was established, and tireless, dedicated missionaries started a long and harrowing struggle to break the caste of slavery and other Indian customs which we, in our civilization, do not condone. To preserve evidences of native culture, a communal house and frieze of totem poles have been restored on Chief Shakes Island.

Lumbering and fishing furnish the economy of this community. Wrangell is a transshipment point for the swift-flowing Stikine River that penetrates the coastal mountains to give access to the interior of northern British Columbia. High-powered, shallow-draft riverboats (with good tourist accommodations) battle a ten-knot current to deliver freight and passengers to Telegraph Creek, 163 miles inland. The trip upstream takes thirty-two hours. Downstream, twelve hours. As a thriller — in complete comfort — it is in a class by itself.

Petersburg, thirty-six miles north of Wrangell, did not spring from the Russian occupation or from the gold rush days. It isn't even a typical Alaskan town. It was started by Norwegian fishermen, and today is still a bit of Norway transplanted to the new state. Most of its citizens are of solid Norwegian stock. They have an economy, an independence and a wealth all their own.

Petersburg has long been a family town. It has fewer bars and liquor stores and more churches per capita than any other community in Alaska. Built on fish, with practically all

the boats owned by Petersburg residents, it has been less
affected by booms and busts than other Alaskan communities.
Logging is becoming a second industry in Petersburg, and
this, too, is a home-owned and home-employed business.

Attractive residences, freshly painted and surrounded by
well-kept lawns and colorful flower gardens, speak well for
the citizenship of these good people. Although there is but
one bank in Petersburg, the deposits in that bank make
Petersburg the wealthiest community per capita in Alaska,
and one of the most independent in the United States.

One hundred miles northwest of Petersburg is Juneau, the
capital of the 49th state. Government, air travel and tourists
constitute its main business.

For years after Joe Juneau and Dick Harris found gold
here in 1880, the community lived a roisterous life. For
nearly forty years thunderous blasts rocked the town as
miners extracted the hard-rock gold. Then, as rising costs
pinched profits into red ink, the blasts were slowly silenced.

Today Juneau is the sedate capital of the new state and
a major tourist attraction. Surrounded by snow-clad mountains, with an icecap of startling grandeur and a live glacier
you can walk on, Juneau is a paradise for the camera fan.

At the State Museum you can see the best in native arti-
facts and handiwork, and the historical relics of the Russian
era. And at the Red Dog Saloon you can return in spirit to
the atmosphere of the gold rush days. In the Bubble Room of
the Baranof Hotel and the night spots of the area your bever-
ages will be served with glacier ice — colder and clearer
than the cubes from your refrigerator.

Less than an hour's flight out of Juneau is Sitka, the old
Russian capital — and today the only way you can get there
is by air. The outstanding attraction of this century-and-a-

half old community is the Russian Orthodox Cathedral of St. Michael. The interior of the richly decorated church, the vestments of its bearded priests, and its ritual carry you back to the days of Baranof.

As they did in the early days, the congregation stands during the hour-long wedding ceremony (there are no seats in the church), and three times during the impressive service the priest asks the bride-to-be, "Are you beholden to any other man?" Of the young man he also inquires at three intervals, "Are you beholden to any other woman?" Only after both have answered "No" three times is the knot tied — permanently.

Ever since the American flag was raised in Sitka in 1867, residents have relished a slow and easy way of life. They are now being drawn into the quickening whirl of the rest of the state, and many of them don't like it.

A new $50,000,000 pulp mill is the cause of the increased tempo. Scores of new homes for employees of the mill are changing the town. Direct freighter service has been established to carry the processed pulp from the Sitka mill to Japan.

At Sitka are located the Alaska Native Service's Mt. Edgecumbe Boarding School — offering high school courses and vocational training to young people of native descent — and the Sheldon Jackson Junior College of the Presbyterian Church.

Just off the waterfront stands the Alaska Pioneers' Home where elderly Sourdoughs — men and women — recall the events of the gold rush days, and rebuild the castles of their dreams.

North of Juneau stretches beautiful Lynn Canal, a natural waterway eighty miles long that ends at Skagway.

Some years ago a visiting Congressman, overwhelmed by free-flowing Alaskan hospitality, confused this God-given waterway with one of the rivers and harbors appropriations he had voted for. Raising his glass to his hosts, he orated clearly, "To you fine citizens of Skagway, let me say, in all candor, that only the digging of the Panama Canal was more important than the digging of your Lynn Canal. I was thrilled to vote for this vital channel."

Thunderous applause and another round of drinks convinced the Congressman he had made the hit of the evening. He had. Alaskans never forgot him.

Skagway thrived as a jump-off spot for the Klondike, and today it lives on the glory of its past. Its most famous resident was Soapy Smith, who made crime a flourishing business before Al Capone was born.

From Skagway the narrow-gauge White Pass & Yukon Railway, built during the Klondike rush, winds perilously over the famous White Pass 112 miles inland to the headwaters of the Yukon River at Whitehorse, where it connects with the Alaska Highway.

Southwest of Skagway, on Lynn Canal, is the village of Haines, which was founded as a Presbyterian mission in 1881. The church still operates Haines House as a mission home for children.

Located at the foot of the Jack Dalton trail to the Klondike, Haines became an active spot during the gold rush. Today Haines is the only community in the Panhandle with a road to the other states — a cut-off road which connects with the Alaska Highway during the summer months.

From Haines the Army has built a pipeline to pump jet fuel and gasoline to the airbases near Fairbanks, and possible mining of iron and other ores in the nearby hills can make this town a thriving port.

Adjacent to Haines is the community of Port Chilkoot, which, prior to World War II, was Uncle Sam's only Army post in Alaska. The impressive old-style Army quarters, which were declared surplus and sold to a group of World War II veterans, now house summertime tourists.

If you fly from the Panhandle to the Big Part of Alaska, and pick a beautiful Chamber of Commerce day, it will be an unrivaled experience of your life. Flying along the coast at 8000 feet you look up at towering mountains, eternally white. You look down on the right side at rivers of ice five, twenty-five and one hundred miles wide — the largest glaciers on the five continents. You look down on the left side at the Pacific Ocean, deceptively quiescent and mirror-blue.

So startling is the grandeur of this panorama that your eyes and your mind grow weary of accepting what you see. You turn to a magazine, or sip a cup of coffee, to give yourself a rest from the emotional impact of God's over-powering handiwork.

Halfway up the Gulf of Alaska is Cordova, near the delta of the Copper River. Once a boom town, it lived on copper for thirty years until the Kennecott mine shut down in 1938, and the Copper River Northwestern Railroad was abandoned.

Cordova is now a fishing community that dreams of greatness. The search for oil nearby is giving citizens great hope for their town. And a study is being made of substantial coal deposits which may be mined for sale in Japan.

If the life's dream of one of Cordova's long-time prominent citizens, John LeFevre, is crowned with success, the completion of the Copper River highway up the spectacular Copper River canyon will emancipate Cordova from its isolation and connect it with the world of wheels and rubber tires.

A scant fifteen minutes west from Cordova is the seaport village of Valdez, which lives on trucking, freighting and tourists. The year-round paved Richardson Highway, which extends from Valdez to Fairbanks, connects with the Alaska Highway and with the Glenn Highway leading to the Matanuska Valley and Anchorage.

Continuing westward your plane crosses Prince William Sound and, far below, at the end of a fiord, you will see a cluster of buildings with a backdrop of glaciers. That is Whittier, a unique institution. It is the only 100 per cent military-owned port under the American flag.

The American government has spent over $50,000,000 building docks, warehouses, a fourteen-story apartment house for military personnel, and a "composite building" that has, under one roof, all offices and facilities for the population of about fifteen hundred persons. Whittier has only about eighty acres of level land, so construction had to go up instead of out.

Your plane continues on across Portage Glacier, then dips its nose steeply down, and ten minutes later you deplane at the Anchorage International Airport.

Anchorage is more like Los Angeles than like a typical Alaskan town. Born in 1914, it is the product of planned parenthood. Its wide streets and rectangular blocks were all laid out on a federal drawing board before a town lot was sold or a false-front building erected. For years it was a quiet town of about twenty-eight hundred residents — the headquarters of the government-owned Alaska Railroad

which runs 471 miles from Seward to Fairbanks. Gold mining
and fishing added to its income, and the Matanuska Colony,
started in 1935, became a new market for Anchorage
merchants.

When Pearl Harbor and the bombing of Dutch Harbor
started an avalanche of military spending in Alaska, the
sleepy little community exploded into the largest city in the
Northland. Today its military installations, as headquarters
of the Alaska Defense Command, are valued at $500,000,000.
The airplane, which redrew the map of Alaska, has made
Anchorage the crossroads of the world, and brought a new
economy to this part of Alaska. The discovery of oil just
forty miles from Anchorage started a new rush north.

Now, with 100,000 residents in its area, Anchorage has a
drive and verve you feel at once. The town is young in
years, young in spirit and impatient in ambition. Name your
interest and you have it here. Cultural groups, an historical
museum, and the new Alaska Methodist University. Anchorage has the finest library in the Northland, a striking structure given to the community by Z. J. Loussac, a Russian
emigrant, in appreciation of the good life Alaska gave him.

Anchorage has more federal and state employees and payroll than does the capital city of Juneau. It is Alaska's medical center — with its Providence Hospital, a huge Air Force
hospital, a 400-bed Native Service Hospital, an Arctic Health
and Research Center, and a mental hospital now in the
planning stage. The community is building an $8,000,000
deep-water port that will further insure Anchorage as the
commercial center of the state.

But you may be hesitant to accept an Alaskan's prej-
udiced viewpoint of the expansive potential of Anchorage.
Benton & Bowles, national advertising agency, sent an ex-

perienced team to Alaska to examine the new state. It reported:

"The biggest part of Alaska's growth will undoubtedly be in the Anchorage area. Anchorage is already the major military and shipping center in the state and the surrounding country contains some of the most promising oil and coal reserves.

"Today Anchorage is comparable in size to Reno, Nevada, and Kankakee, Illinois. By 1968 it will probably compare with Fort Wayne, Indiana, and Des Moines, Iowa. And by 1978 Anchorage should be as important a market as Providence, Rhode Island, or Denver, Colorado, are today."

This study says that Anchorage will have 238,000 residents in 1968 and 725,000 in 1978.

Fifty miles north of Anchorage, by paved highway, is the Matanuska Valley. Its prosperity is evident in the progressive town of Palmer, the heart of this fertile valley. Dairy processing, agricultural development, coal mining and the search for oil are giving the Matanuska area a stepped-up tempo.

One hundred and twenty miles south of Anchorage, on Resurrection Bay, is the seaport town of Seward, the southern terminus of the Alaska Railroad. For forty years Seward's principal livelihood was the transfer of passengers and freight from steamer to rail.

When the passengers took to the air and flew direct from Seattle to their destinations in Alaska, Seward took it on the chin. But the highway from the other states to Anchorage was extended down the Kenai Peninsula, and Seward took on new life as a tourist center.

A new commercial fishing industry has mushroomed in the area with the discovery that the bottom of the sea was crawling with delicious, large-size shrimp. And sports fishing for salmon in Resurrection Bay is becoming big business.

West of Seward is the homestead land of the Kenai. This fertile acreage and the Kenai's big game refuge are being crisscrossed by seismic crews feverishly probing the depths for oil structures. The village of Kenai, an old Russian settlement, is only a few miles from the site of the first oil strike, and residents are burning candles for the sign they have erected: KENAI, THE OIL CAPITAL OF ALASKA.

Homer, at the end of the road on the Kenai Peninsula, stands to prosper greatly if oil spouts in this part of Alaska. Homer has salmon fishing, crab and shrimp processing, hunting, farming, and some of the most beautiful scenery in the new state. Now that the highway from Anchorage to Homer is being paved, tourists will add an economic fillip to this community.

Kodiak is an hour's flight from Anchorage, or about twenty minutes by air from Homer. Kodiak is the oldest town in Alaska, and dispensing early Russian history is an avocation of the townspeople.

Kodiak is headquarters for the 17th Naval District, and from here picket ships and radar planes cover the area to the Aleutians and Hawaii. About half of Kodiak's economy stems from the naval base.

Fresh freezing and canning of Kodiak king crab is becoming big business — now soaring to $6,000,000 annually. White-topped Howard Wakefield is Mr. Big of Alaska's king crab industry, and through his promotion and salesmanship this delicacy of the sea is becoming known through the country.

When shrimp was discovered recently in the waters near

Kodiak, shrimp packers from New Orleans rushed north to study the potential. Excitedly they reported that one boat could harvest as much shrimp in one day near Kodiak as five boats could catch in five days off the coast of Louisiana.

Kodiak Island has cattle ranches and the biggest bear on earth. Big game hunters have found that a trophy Kodiak bruin usually tips the checkbook at about $2000. Every year about two hundred of these gigantic carnivora are mounted, or end their days as rugs in the guest house — the finest objects in the world to stub your toe on when going to the bathroom at three in the morning.

To reach Fairbanks, in Central Alaska, you can fly, drive, or ride the Alaska Railroad from Anchorage. En route you view 20,320-foot-high Mt. McKinley and other peaks which are higher than the mountains in any other state. As the mountains gradually diminish into the flat reaches of the Interior, you arrive at Fairbanks on the banks of the Chena River.

Fairbanks started life as a lusty gold camp back in 1904. Today it is probably the most typical Alaskan town you will find. It has log cabins, dog teams and grizzled prospectors. But it also has tall apartment houses, sports cars, parking meters and supermarkets.

Twenty years ago Fairbanks boasted twenty-five hundred permanent residents, most of them dependent on gold for their livelihood. Then Uncle Sam decided to build a cold-weather testing station for airplanes just outside of town, and the military arrived.

With World War II, this station mushroomed into Ladd Air Force Base, and the government poured $50,000,000 into this installation and into Eielson Air Force Base twenty-six miles farther south. Eielson has runways three miles long which can jet intercontinental bombers into the Arctic sky and over the Pole at a moment's notice.

Fairbanks has grown ten times in size in twenty years. Though its biggest payroll is the military, there is still some gold mining in the vicinity, and the expanding University of Alaska five miles distant brings a steady income to the town.

Fairbanks is tourist-conscious and plays up its Winter Carnival, its Midnight Sun baseball game on the longest day of the year, and its riverboat trip down the Chena River — the only place in Alaska where you can still ride a stern-wheeler.

Fairbanks, more than any other Alaskan town, has intangibles that reveal the warmth of Alaska. It is one of the few communities where you can still meet some of the Northland's colorful personalities — the real Golden Heart of Alaska.

Queen of the Northland is Mrs. Eva McGown, city hostess of Fairbanks who, most Alaskans agree, is the Bridie Ballantyne of Edna Ferber's *Ice Palace*. Eva, who has her own TV program, is a friend of world travelers, homesick GIs, bedless tourists and ailing Sourdoughs. Her brogue is County Cork, her heart is big, and she remembers nothing but the best of everyone.

Then there is the incomparable Dave Adler, philosopher and bookseller, who has as fine a selection of volumes for sale as you will find in a metropolitan bookshop. But more people come into Adler's Book Shop to talk with Dave than to buy books. Dave has a sharp mind, a keen wit and a prodigious memory. He rarely needs to refer to publishers' catalogues, recalling from memory all pertinent facts on thousands of volumes requested by his customers.

An important figure in the land of permafrost is Frank

Mapleton, long-time Alaskan and head of one of the world's unique public utility systems. "With a circulating water system, and a freeze-proof sewage system, Fairbanks has proved that a big city can be built and operated efficiently any place in the permafrost regions of the Arctic," Frank stated. "We also have a modern electrical power plant, a weather-proof telephone system, and central steam heat for the downtown area."

Fairbanks is home to more pioneers of the gold rush era than any other Alaskan town, and even at 50 below zero these old-timers religiously attend the meetings of Igloo No. 4, Pioneers of Alaska.

Westward from Fairbanks, about five hundred miles over tundra, rivers and mountains, on the edge of the Bering Sea, is Nome. The only way you can travel to the Seward Peninsula is by air, but Nomeites hope it won't be long before Highway 97 is completed across the vast Interior to connect their community with the rest of Alaska and the other states.

At the turn of the century Nome was a rip-roaring gold-mining community of ten thousand souls, but in recent years the entire economy of this district has been flipped like a pancake on a hot griddle.

Nome is still the center for such gold mining as remains, but military installations along the coast and the DEW Line are helping to bring new cash into the community. If plans of Alaska Airlines are approved, tourist flights will take off from Nome across Bering Strait to Siberia.

As in other parts of the new state, Nome is finding tourists the easiest cash crop to harvest. In this part of Alaska the sightseer really gets his money's worth. Eskimo women parade Front Street in calico-covered parkas with sleeping babes framed in their hoods, and Eskimo men from nearby

Diomede and King islands sit under their oomiaks and carve ivory figures and letter openers.

While tourists are discovering the natives and their civilization, the natives are becoming fascinated with life around the globe. Nome is the smallest town in the world with its own TV station, and the community's population (three-fourths native) follows international news reports and current cowboy shows.

Kotzebue, a picturesque native village north of Nome, is a regular overnight stop on Wien Alaska Airlines' Eskimo-land tours, and the delightful Eskimo people entertain with native dances, blanket tossing and skinboat rides.

Kotzebue and Point Barrow are crowded in the spring with big game hunters who seek to bag the vanishing polar bear. The hire of a guide and/or bush pilot to fly out over the Arctic ice for hundreds of miles and spot a bear is to-day's routine of polar bear hunting.

Once the bear is sighted, the plane lands on the ice nearby, the nimrod steps out, and usually, without too much trouble, adds another trophy to his collection. At the present rate of hunting, live polar bears will soon be attractions to be found only in zoos.

No part of Alaska is changing more than the Arctic. It was only a few short years ago that the first talking movie was shown in Point Barrow. The technicolor picture opened with a cargo netload of fruit being lowered from a ship to the dock. The Eskimo kids in the front row made a break for the screen to grab the fruit before they realized it was just a movie.

In the back of the room stood a weather-worn Eskimo grandmother, bent low with the hardships of the uncompromising Arctic way of life. Her eyes were glued to the screen, and, in a slow, plaintive whisper — almost a dirge-like wail — she repeated over and over again, "Ah-yahh, Ahhh-yahhh." This can't be true!

Today there are regular flights of passenger and freight planes to Barrow, and the village at the top of the world has two modest tourist hotels, run by Eskimos.

Tomorrow — or soon thereafter — roads will be built throughout the Eskimo empire. When that happens, the annual summer potlatch at Point Barrow will have other things to talk about besides this year's crop of babies, how many whales were harpooned this spring, and how much money Papa made on the DEW Line.

At present, the Eskimo with the biggest outboard motor is the envied kingpin of the community. But when the road is opened from Detroit to Point Barrow, Joe Eskimo, who arrives at the top of the continent in a Michigan Special complete with soaring tailfins, will steal the show. Until bigger fins are built on bigger cars, he will be No. 1 on the social register.

4

For Military Personnel Only

Fʀᴏᴍ ᴛʜᴇ ᴍᴏᴍᴇɴᴛ ᴛʜᴀᴛ Jᴏʜɴ ᴀɴᴅ ʜɪs ғᴀᴍɪʟʏ heard rumors that they might be transferred to Alaska, condolences came pouring in.

"How awful! I hear you have to stay indoors all year round, and there is absolutely nothing to do!"

"All that ice and snow! And no shops or places to buy *anything*. We'll save you our magazines and newspapers, old boy."

"Imagine having to wear long underwear, Mary! And no cocktail dresses or formal wear. Won't it be ghastly?"

And so on. And so on.

John's was not an isolated case. Fully ninety out of every hundred military personnel transferred to Alaska don't have the foggiest idea of what they're coming to, and do little to prepare themselves for their two years up north. They decide to dislike the place, to sit it out, and in the interim get their livers into an awful state. Before their transport sails they are already counting the months, days, hours and minutes until they can rotate Stateside again.

In spite of the number of troops and Navy personnel who have been stationed up here since the war, the idea of Alaska as a last frontier covered with a permanent mantle of snow, ice, Eskimos and polar bears still predominates among the armed forces.

Otherwise skeptical and rational individuals will accept as gospel the "true facts" on Alaska as told by experts who have never been closer to the Arctic Circle than the Mason-Dixon Line. One field grade officer arrived at Elmendorf Air Force Base, near Anchorage, with his wife, three small children, and four cases of toilet tissue. He had been told that Alaska was so primitive that even old Sears, Roebuck catalogues sold at a premium.

Another family arrived with a station wagon half full of Tide, and other newcomers have foregone part of their household weight allowance to bring cases of canned goods and other foodstuffs to help see them through their tour of duty.

Soldiers and airmen have sold their cars at a sacrifice or have put them into Stateside storage to wait longingly for the day when they could drive again.

And families have looked tearfully for a good home for their pets, because the poor animals would not be able to live through an Alaskan winter.

Since statehood put the spotlight on Alaska, journalists have descended on the Northland by the dozens, and periodicals are beginning to give a truer picture of life up here. To help indoctrinate service personnel who are coming north, the Pentagon bought 200,000 reprints of "The Story of Alaska" from *U.S. News & World Report* — an excellent short course on understanding the state of Alaska. Military personnel at most bases are given literature on Alaska, but, as one Alaskan information officer said, it looks as if the majority of them don't bother to read it.

Unfortunately the hundreds of personal adventure books on Alaska that you will find in your library and at the bookstores will be of no value to you; that is, if you want facts that will be helpful. These books, you will soon learn after you have been to Alaska and have seen things for yourself, have been written to entertain rather than to inform. After all, "Living in the Arctic with the Eskimos" and "Traveling the Yukon in a Canoe" will hardly prepare you for living on a modern military base in Alaska.

Don't be misled by all the hardship stories you hear from military personnel stationed in Alaska during World War II. There is no comparison between conditions then and now.

For instance, if you'll pick up a road map of Alaska from your favorite oil company, and study the road system of the new state, you'll probably say, "Look at all the blacktopped roads! Let's not sell our car, let's take it along. We can even drive to the Yukon River!"

And to put your mind at ease, you can buy every major standard brand or label of merchandise, apparel, jewelry, food, drugs, sporting goods and whiskey that you can in the south 48 states. The PXs, the commissaries, and the stores and shops in town can supply you with everything you need or want. Retail prices on many nationally advertised brands of merchandise are virtually the same as they are Outside, so there is no need for loading up on anything before coming north.

Every base has row after row of modern, steam-heated apartments and residences for married personnel, although quarters are not always immediately available. Bases have all the club and recreational facilities enjoyed elsewhere, including golf courses, ski runs, well-equipped gymnasiums and indoor swimming pools. The social life is just as vigorous, if not more so, than at Stateside bases.

The larger communities in Alaska all have TV stations,

radio stations and local newspapers. Seattle papers are flown in daily, and the air-mail editions of *Time* and *Newsweek* arrive the same day subscribers get theirs in the other states.

Unless an Army wife is a complete outdoor enthusiast she will have much more use for cocktail and formal wear than she ever will for woolies. Children need snow suits and lined boots, but no warmer clothing than they would wear in upstate New York or in northern Minnesota. Homes and schools are usually kept so warm in the winter time that even sweaters are unnecessary indoors.

As for pets, dogs are so plentiful here that several towns have kennel clubs which hold their own point shows licensed by the American Kennel Club. The canine population includes Chihuahuas, Pomeranians, boxers, Afghans, French poodles and all other breeds. And pet shops up here carry Siamese cats, parakeets, turtles, monkeys, rabbits and tropical fish.

It is not true, as one serviceman heard, that "they only sell Fords in Alaska." Up here you can buy every make of car from Crosley to Cadillac. Sports cars are just as well represented up here as they are in the old 48 states — and the Volkswagen is especially popular with residents because its air-cooled engine doesn't require anti-freeze during the winter season. The highly decorated used-car lots, with "bargains" and come-ons, are plentiful in the Northland, and Alaska has its share of teen-agers' jalopies.

Many military families drive to Alaska over the Alaska Highway, letting Uncle, through the AG's office, pick up the tab. Some fly north, but most depart from San Francisco or Seattle on a military transport. Since Uncle Sam is not interested in the tourist aspects of the trip, your transport heads directly out to sea and doesn't make any landfalls until you reach your destination. If you are Navy, your transport will sail straight out across the North Pacific for Kodiak, and all you will see are gulls, goonies and a good portion of the biggest ocean in the world.

Practically all military personnel who come to Alaska will be stationed at Army and Air Force bases near Anchorage and Fairbanks, and they will see nothing of Alaska until their ship approaches the port of Whittier on Prince William Sound. Alaskans feel that this is a lousy introduction to the Northland, as Whittier is known as a spot where it can rain all summer and snow all winter. But if you arrive on a rare Chamber of Commerce day you will be greeted by blue skies, white clouds, high mountains, glistening glaciers — and two huge skyscrapers.

You board a special blue and gold streamliner of the Alaska Railroad and in five minutes you're in a long tunnel with a mountain and a glacier over your head. Emerging from the other side, nine times out of ten you will meet sunshine — or weather opposite that at Whittier.

Another tunnel and you are on the shore of Turnagain Arm, a branch of Cook Inlet. During certain seasons of the year you can see literally dozens of moose in this area.

Your train skirts Turnagain Arm, and soon you arrive in Anchorage — about a two-hour trip. The size and modern appearance of this community will surprise you. If you arrive with battalion replacements, the train will probably take you directly to Fort Richardson.

The routine of reporting in, assignment to casual quarters, then permanent assignment, are no different here from Fort Monroe or Fort Lewis.

If you are assigned to Ladd or Eielson bases near Fairbanks, you will probably go north on the Alaska Railroad streamliner, a scenic twelve-hour ride through the heartland of Alaska, with Mt. McKinley looking down on you for half the distance. The Central district of Alaska is hotter in summer and colder in winter than is the Anchorage area. But if you can live in the northern half of the lower 48 states, you can survive in this part of Alaska.

In fact, most personnel find that living in Alaska is little different from living Outside. The winter is a little longer, but no colder than many Stateside stations. Although there is snow on the ground for five to six months in the Big Part of Alaska, the sun shines a good deal of the time, and there is plenty of skiing, skating and dog team riding.

Alaskans drive their cars all winter long. A heater inside the car, a headbolt heater for cold weather starting, and snow tires for winter driving are SOP for Alaska. Chains for emergency use are the only extras needed. Military personnel who bring their cars north have a wonderful opportunity to see the wonders of the new state. They can drive to Seward and Homer on the Kenai Peninsula, to Valdez on Prince William Sound, and even to Dawson City and Whitehorse on the Canadian side.

One young Army officer, who has probably learned as much about Alaska in one tour of duty as some Sourdoughs have in a lifetime, was quick to tell his men, "If you want to gain anything out of your stay in Alaska, then get off the base. You won't absorb any of the flavor of the country, or get to know the people, by circulating around the service clubs, the PX and the post movies."

This young officer practiced what he preached. He had been to the R & R camps at Lake Louise and King Salmon, and he'd hunted and fished all over Alaska. He volunteered to go on air searches with the CAP and saw a lot of Alaska while looking for downed fliers. "I met a swell bunch of Alaskans this way, too," he remarked.

The Miners Short Course, given by the University of Alaska Extension Service, got him all excited about prospecting, and he took off on a number of gold-panning expeditions into the mountains. He met up with some of the dog mushers in town, and one of them let him run five dogs in a beginner's race. "I was stiff for a week," he laughed, "but it was worth it.

"Some of the men on the Base belong to service clubs in town like Rotary, Lions and Kiwanis, and they have met some very wonderful people," he said. "Alaskans are anxious to make friends with the military if they're willing to give something of themselves in return."

To find out something about the history of the country, this young man joined the local historical society and remarked, "I've got enough yarns of the early days to start a lecture series on Alaska when I go Outside. But frankly, I've enjoyed Alaska so much that I've asked for a six months' extension."

Though this young officer was interested in more activities than most people, it's getting more and more common up North to hear military personnel say, "We've extended." There just hasn't been enough time for them to see and do all they've wanted to.

"When I got my orders to come to Alaska I'd have sold out for a handful of Confederate currency," one Air Force man confessed. "But honestly, the family and I have enjoyed our tour up here so much that when I get out we're coming back as civilians."

A growing number feel the same way. Some military personnel have already bought property and have made their business connections so they'll be ready to start right in as contributing members of the new state. Others, by the score, have homesteaded while on duty up here — looking ahead to their retirement.

"Alaska gets under the skin of a lot of us," one soldier admitted. Some of the hard-shelled haters of a tour of duty in Alaska, who arrive with a chip on the shoulder, leave the Northland with genuine regret. They carry away an affection for the Land of the Midnight Sun and its people that is hard to put into words.

A gruff spit-and-polish three-star general had tears in his eyes when some four hundred resident Alaskans turned out to shake him by the hand and wish him godspeed as he was rotating. Both he and his wife love Alaska and would like to return.

"About the only person in the service who refuses to like Alaska," a ranking officer remarked at a cocktail party, "is the soul who was conceived in a West Side bachelor's apartment, grew up in East Side night clubs, hates the smell of fresh air, and has reached the sublime heights when mentioned in a Broadway gossip column."

For this character — male or female — Alaska will be a miserable experience.

But for those who love fun, who can thrill to an orchid sunrise on a snowclad peak, whose ears are tuned to the whisper of a mallard's wings — Alaska will be a short tour of pleasant duty.

5

The Personal Side of Alaska

FOUR YEARS AGO BILL MERRITT, A SUCCESSFUL Fairbanks life insurance underwriter, and his wife, Sue, were fed up with Alaska. They were sick of coping with winter temperatures that swooped to 50 below, and decided that life for their two young daughters and infant son would be easier in sunny California.

Last year, with the family enlarged by another small boy, the Merritts were back in Alaska. They bought a home in Anchorage, outfitted four young Merritts with snow suits and boots, and, to quote Bill, "started living again."

"Sure, we made money down south, and life was a lot simpler," he stated. "But where's the challenge? Life in the other states follows a pattern and everybody conforms.

"Alaskans live in a wider world. They have more interests and more enthusiasm. They accomplish things and change things. I want my kids to live in a land with a future — a future they can help to build."

Alaskans are, by nature, liberals, or they would not have come to this demanding frontier to get away from the fetters and bondage of tradition, caste and overpopulation. They are people who want to do their own thinking, make their own decisions, and determine their own destinies.

In Alaska there are few precedents to follow, so Alaskans are not bound by rigid convention. They get things done — and ask questions afterwards.

In Anchorage, a bachelor postman by the name of George Byer dreamed up and carried through a project of flying a Texas high school football team to Anchorage to play with the local boys. (Texas won.) He was instrumental in getting Anchorage the All-America City award, and he has become nationally known as the sparkplug of Anchorage. George is an influential member of the local Chamber of Commerce and of the Alaska World Affairs Council.

Six-foot-one, and soft-spoken, George says, "A guy has to give something of himself to justify his existence in our society today. And nowhere in the world does a man have such an opportunity to give of himself — and to get more accomplished in a short time — than right here in Alaska."

Alaska is a new land, a raw land, and the surface has only been scratched. Alaskans work hard because there is so much to be accomplished and because, seemingly, everything must all be done in one lifetime.

Visitors to the Northland are amazed at the number of man hours Alaskans put in every day, and invariably ask, "Do all Alaskans work this hard?"

The answer is "Yes." A young couple may be living in a basement, and building their own home on evenings and week ends, but the wife is president of the PTA, and the husband is on the city council, the zoning commission or the park board. Because Alaska has no retired or leisure class to take over its civic duties and charitable drives, young businessmen and their wives automatically add these activities to their daily routine.

Alaskans are terrific joiners, and every Alaskan community has one or more of Rotary, Lions, Kiwanis, Masons, Elks, Moose, the Legion and all auxiliaries. There are so many women's organizations that it's a rare Alaskan housewife who isn't active in at least three or four. Children have Boy Scouts, Girl Scouts, Camp Fire Girls, 4-H Clubs, Future Farmers of America, Little League Baseball, and extracurricular school activities.

Alaskans don't feel that joining takes away their individuality. They join for social life and they join to accomplish things in the community they couldn't get done alone.

Alaska's population is young, and its birth rate is the highest in the land. Most of Alaska's new citizens are born in modern hospitals — and are among the healthiest in the nation. Alaskan children miss fewer days of school because of illness than do children in the other states.

With the influx of population have come more doctors and dentists, and larger communities have pediatricians, heart specialists, orthopedists and orthodontists. The Department of Health has classes for expectant mothers, free child clinics, and flying doctors and nurses who cover the hinterland to give shots, make examinations, and dispense medical advice.

If you have been offered a job in Alaska, and have been holding back for fear your children would not receive a proper education, you can dismiss this worry at once. Your children will attend some of the newest and best-equipped schools in the country. The constant complaint of youngsters transferring from Outside is "They make us work too hard."

Alaskans, college-educated well above the national average, have always demanded the best in schooling for their children. For years, over fifty per cent of the entire Alaskan governmental budget has been earmarked for education, and parents pack the local school board meetings to be sure the money is well spent.

The Alaska Board of Education pays the highest wages in the country, but it is a particular employer. Teachers must match up to a high criterion of training, experience and personal qualities. There is no color or creed barrier in Alaska, and Negro teachers are employed in a number of schools throughout the state.

No one has been more astonished at the caliber of Alaskan schools than two planeloads of Methodist district superintendents who arrived in Anchorage several years ago to start a fund drive for Alaska's Methodist University. To hear them tell it, they'd pictured Anchorage as a Sergeant Preston town, with a bunch of log cabins and a lot of frontier atmosphere.

After they toured Anchorage's $5,300,000 ultramodern high school — complete with terrazzo floors, illuminated aquariums, a gymnasium with two full-sized basketball courts and bleachers to hold five thousand spectators, and an auditorium with a stage capable of handling any New York production even to Radio City Music Hall shows — the entire delegation was rocked back on its heels.

Plans for modest AMU buildings were revised, and a new concept of what the liberal arts college would look like was unveiled several months later. The university's president, progressive Dr. Donald Ebright, is determined that the Alaska Methodist University (which will open in Anchorage in the fall of 1960) will match the high standards of other Methodist-sponsored colleges throughout the nation.

Modern schools have been built in practically every Alaskan town. In Fairbanks and Anchorage, where the population is soaring, construction of schools is an annual event.

The reasoning behind de luxe schools in the Northland is psychological. Alaskan children do not have the opportunity to live with the inspirational architecture of great universities, museums, libraries and fine arts buildings found in the older states. Modern, well-equipped school buildings inspire a pride of ownership in the students, and make them strive for the better things of life.

In Alaska, too, school buildings must serve the community as multipurpose structures for concerts, for meetings, for recreation and for a score of other activities so essential to the character development of its young citizens.

Whether you live in one of the larger towns, or in a community way out in the boondocks, your children will receive the same course of instruction. Practically all Alaskan schools are accredited by the Northwest Association of Secondary and Higher Schools, so students have little difficulty in transferring Outside or going on to college.

If your job takes you to a remote area where there are no schools, and not enough children to warrant one (the state must furnish a teacher for ten or more children in an area) the state will supply you with the Calvert Correspondence Course of Elementary Education. A number of children living at remote navigational beam sites are receiving their entire grammar school education by correspondence, and tests made with these youngsters have shown that a good many educated by mail are superior students.

Several Alaskan towns have parochial schools, and the federal government operates boarding schools for children of native descent. A junior college run by the Presbyterian church is located in Sitka.

Just a scant hundred miles south of the Arctic Circle, near Fairbanks, is the University of Alaska — a fast-growing liberal arts college which exerts a profound cultural and intellectual influence on life in the Northland. So many young men and women are applying for admittance to America's farthest north university that housing is at a premium and campus facilities are being expanded rapidly.

The University of Alaska is a land-grant school which confers degrees in seventeen colleges and departments, plus advanced degrees in a number of fields. Its six-weeks summer school attracts students and teachers from all over the nation. The university also operates, for college credit, community colleges in Anchorage, Juneau, Ketchikan and Palmer.

The university has a top-flight faculty, purposely small classes for more individual instruction, and undergraduate activities and societies found in Outside colleges.

Much credit for the high standards of the university is due to its president, Dr. Ernest Patty, who knows Alaska as well as he knows his students. Dr. Patty joined the staff of the embryo college in 1922 as its first dean of the school of mines. Eighteen years later he resigned to mine gold. He made a sizable fortune and was ready to retire in 1952 when the board of regents tapped him to be the U. of A.'s third president.

The university's modern plant is climaxed by a new $4,000,-000 multipurpose building, and some of the most beautiful men's and women's dormitories to be seen on any campus. An internationally important Geophysical Institute, which is the nucleus for research studies of the polar and sub-Arctic regions, has brought world-famous scientists to the university.

Since the earliest days, when the missionaries came to far-away Alaska, religion has profoundly influenced the lives of the pioneers on the last frontier.

As one old-timer wrote, "There is something about the vastness and the majesty of this great land that appeals to the spiritual qualities within man. No one can stand before the awesome splendor of towering Mt. McKinley and fail of inspiration. No one can watch the rushing sweep of the Northern Lights and doubt the existence of a supreme order to this universe. Perhaps it is the insignificance of man against the canopy of heaven that causes him to look upward. And look upward he does."

This spiritual feeling manifests itself in religious organizations on the frontier. In every town and hamlet there are churches and groups with their own rituals of religious observance. Anchorage alone has eighty-six groups and congregations, ranging from apostolic faiths which hold meetings on the curb in front of the bars to the most conservative denominations whose structures are landmarks in the town. There is, as yet, no synagogue in Alaska, although a Jewish congregation has recently been formed in Anchorage.

For many years, much of the social and recreational life of the Northland has revolved around the church. Women's societies, youth organizations, family dinners, bazaars, and summer camps for young people have brightened life on the frontier.

Out in the lonesome bush, the radio brings religion to all who will listen. This solace, originating in Salt Lake, Kansas City, Long Beach or Anchorage often provides the invisible helping hand that pulls a family through a wilderness crisis.

Thousands of Alaskans have been helped physically and spiritually by the selfless workers of the Salvation Army. "It's tough enough being stranded Outside without a dime or a friend," said Brigadier C. C. Clitheroe, for years one of the Army's best beloved workers in Alaska. "But when that happens up here, an additional two thousand miles away from home — it is well to have God and the Salvation Army on your side."

In the last few years, the physical effort of living in the Northland has become simplified. Housing is no longer the desperate problem it was at the close of World War II. New homes with modern conveniences have taken much of the drudgery out of northern living. Along with new homes, every major town has a number of recently constructed apartment houses, and thousands of residents of the Northland are living in well-insulated trailers and trailer homes.

Though living space may not be critical, the cost comes high. Many a newcomer has practically suffered a stroke when a bright-eyed real estate salesman quoted him the price of a new home in the sub-Arctic.

Roughly, construction in the Big Part of Alaska runs from $25 to $30 per square foot (compared with $13 per square foot in southern California) and the closer you get to the North Pole, the higher go the prices. Unless your home has at least four inches of good insulation all around, you are not only heating your house, you're heating the universe and keeping the fuel oil dealer in Cadillacs.

If you decide to rent a modern apartment, be prepared to pay about double what you're paying Outside. Ketchikan, Juneau, Anchorage and Fairbanks have new skyscraper apartments, along with a considerable number of less pretentious apartments and flats which attract the family trade.

The cost of moving north will make a much bigger dent in your pocketbook than you ever believed possible, and newcomers have found that living in a hotel while house hunting can get mighty expensive. Also, hotel rooms in Anchorage and Fairbanks are at a premium the year around, and it is practically impossible to find one during the summer tourist season.

Food also comes high. Many a newcomer has almost decided to quit eating after his first trip to the supermarket. It's not unusual to pay sixty cents for an airborne head of lettuce, and a bunch of celery costs close to a dollar during the winter. Apples and bananas weigh up to about twenty cents apiece. To many Alaskan children, fruit is much more of a treat than a candy bar.

Living off the land is a fiction for most people — especially when that land is frozen six months out of the year. Contrary to what you've heard, you don't just step out your back door and shoot your locker full of moose and caribou. Many a housewife has discovered that friend husband's moose has cost about double per pound what they would have paid for prime beef. And moose can get pretty tiresome as a steady diet.

A car is a necessity in the larger communities because bus service is limited and taxi fares are prohibitive for a commuter. Sub-zero temperatures and unpaved roads age a car fast. And gasoline averages ten to fifteen cents more per gallon than in the other states.

When the wife of an Army sergeant from Georgia visited a beauty shop in Fairbanks for the first time, the shock of the prices almost straightened out her new curl.

"I'd be scared stiff to tell my husband how much I paid for this permanent," she confided to the operator.

But the beautician, also an Army wife, came back with "Did your husband tell you how much more he is getting up here every payday?"

The military and the federal agencies pay higher salaries in Alaska. So does private industry, and these publicized higher wages entice many persons north. But in most cases, higher living costs eat up the differential, and a man may find he's worse off financially than he was back home. Much of the high standard of living enjoyed in Alaska is the result of both man and wife being employed.

But high prices are not as much a deterrent to life in the Northland as are the intangible psychological factors.

A New York roving reporter asked a number of on-the-street New Yorkers if they would come to Alaska if they got a lot more money. One man answered, "I would have to know a lot of answers before making my decision. How are social conditions? I don't mean wild times or things like that. I mean, can a guy keep from going crazy? I gotta know before I'd go."

This young man put his finger on the psychological drawback to living in the Northland. In Alaska you have to be able to live with yourself to an extent not known Outside. You can't drive fifty miles to a big city, kick up your heels and blow off steam. Alaska has no big cities — the largest, Anchorage, has a population under 100,000. To get away from it all, you'd have to take a plane to Seattle or Minneapolis.

Social life and entertainment are geared to a small orbit. In most communities you see the same people every day. You know their stories by heart. They know all about you. You exchange dinners, watch the same TV programs, go to the same churches and attend the same Chamber of Commerce banquets.

Alaskans take this semi-isolation as part of the way of life in the Northland. They do much of their entertaining in their homes, make their own joys and pleasures, and read, read, read.

Many Alaskans find their outlets in cultural pursuits. Mary

Hale, wife of an Anchorage physician, conducts a magnificent community chorus which has appeared on the Ed Sullivan show. She also originated and directs an annual festival of music featuring Robert Shaw, Julius Herford and a variety of world-famed vocalists and instrumentalists. Anchorage has a symphony orchestra, five little theater groups, writers' clubs, artist societies and Arthur Murray dance instructors. Other communities have similar activities.

Those who live in outlying villages and on isolated homesteads find the going harder — both physically and psychologically. The heaviest burden is on the youngsters and teenagers who crave outlets for their energies, but find little constructive to do in the villages. A weekly movie, a soda fountain with a jukebox, a lunch counter hangout adopted by the kids — this is the social swing.

"We find that some people forget the essentials of civilization out in the bush," a Department of Health consultant said. "For instance, a coffee can under the bed is not a hygienic substitute for a good privy. Lack of personal discipline often causes homesteaders to let down. The men quit shaving and neglect haircuts. The women literally and figuratively take off their girdles.

"The best advice we can give any person coming north is, 'Bring your civilization with you,'" the consultant said. "Plan to live up here on as high a plane as you did Outside. Establish a routine of living and stick to it.

"That old bromide, cleanliness is next to godliness, is a sharp principle of life in Alaska," she went on. "Your mental outlook is improved by a hot bath and clean clothes."

One of the results of too much isolation in Alaska has been a king-sized consumption of alcohol. It started with the earliest trappers and miners, and even today Alaska's liquor consumption is reported to be five times the national average.

But because of this statement, don't turn to the family and say, "That settles it. We are not going to Alaska. It says right here that it is a land of drunkards. And we don't want to associate with people who have liquor on their breath all the time."

Let us offer a conclusion that most Alaskans will support. The person who has an alcoholic problem anywhere in the other states will have a bigger problem up here. Except for a few native communities which are dry, liquor flows freely, even at 60 below.

There are relatively few homes where a bottle isn't kept for friends who drop in, for a cocktail before dinner, or for just ordinary medicinal purposes. Much entertaining is done with liquor accompaniment.

This situation is not unique to Alaska. But because Alaska's population is small, you're closer to it up here.

In spite of its disadvantages, Alaska is fast becoming a land of modern homes and families. Today's young men heading north are bringing along their wives and kiddies, and Alaska is no longer the happy hunting ground for adventurous women it was a few years back. Where the ratio of men to women was fifty to one in the gold mining days, it is now down to sixteen males to every ten females and the gap is closing fast.

This switch to family life has brought the curtain down on one of the last vestiges of the crimson days of the Yukon. The first state legislature abolished Alaska's B-Girls — the lassies in the night spots who got paid on the basis of how much liquor they could entice their male customers to buy.

Gone is the once well-patronized Row on Fourth Avenue in Fairbanks. Here the charming doxies dispensed liquor and conversation at a dollar a shot and companionship at a slightly higher fee.

Gone, too, is the famous Ketchikan institution. Out over Ketchikan Creek, up which thousands and thousands of salmon swim each fall, was a row of chummy little houses — the rendezvous for loggers, sailors, fishermen and other gentlemen on the prowl.

Gone are the houses. Gone are the girls. And no longer may it be said that "The Creek" exists where salmon and fishermen alike enjoyed going upstream to spawn.

Progress — and urban renewal programs — have taken over.

6

So You're Driving to Alaska!

THE ALASKA HIGHWAY IS THE MOST MALIGNED piece of roadway in the Western Hemisphere.

It's been given the needle by lecturers and copywriters, and painted as a combination of the hazards of climbing Mt. McKinley and the perils of touring behind the Iron Curtain. The supreme test of a car or tire is its ability to come through with flying colors over the tortuous northern thoroughfare.

"Not even a 900-mile detour could stop Mish-Mash tires on this rubber-killing Alaska Highway," one ad stated. And to prove it, there's a picture of a truck and trailer running taillight deep through a mountain stream as Mish-Mash tires grit their treads and come through smiling.

Another supreme bit of fanciful copy, which took up a double-page spread in one of our largest-circulation magazines, showed an automobile driving Alaska-ward over a by-pass road *two and one-half years before that bypass road was built.*

If you ask any Alaskan how he managed to chug his way north — or south — under such perilous conditions, you are due for quick disillusionment. His description of the highway will probably be so disenchanting that you'll say, a little dispiritedly, "Why, that sounds just like driving anywhere else."

Cars of every description, make and model have traversed the Alaska Highway. As one newsman put it, "You see as many varieties of foreign sports cars in Anchorage as you do in Palm Springs."

A Juneau schoolteacher drove north in an Isetta, and an Anchorage man finally got so fed up with all the stories about the perilous highway that he drove his 1930 Model A Ford to Milwaukee to dispel the rumors. He was somewhat put out when the Canadians made him post a bond on his vintage model — especially when they told him the five dollars was to "sweep the wreckage to one side." He had no engine trouble, and made the trip without even getting a new squeak in the chassis.

No matter what the make or model, it's a cinch to spot a car that's just driven over the Alaska Highway. Like birds of a feather, many of them carry luggage racks on top and/or trailers behind, are well supplied with stickers that say "WEL-COME TO CANADA," have mesh bug-catchers shielding the front, and their headlights and bumpers are taped against flying gravel.

About forty per cent of the people coming to Alaska today drive over the Alaska Highway. But as the highway proper does not officially start until "way up yonder," a thousand or so miles from your home town, let's start your trip back in the old south 48 states.

If you're from the East, the South or the Midwest you'll head for Great Falls, Montana, your jumping-off base for the far north. Here, if you're wise, you'll have your car completely serviced before you turn your windshield toward the Midnight Sun.

From Great Falls you'll drive 891 miles in a northwesterly direction, through Calgary and Edmonton, to Dawson Creek, British Columbia, the "Mile Zero" of the Alaska Highway. This wheat-growing community on the prairie became the starting point of the Alaska Highway back in 1942, because it was the farthest north end of rail transportation. As a war emergency, the highway was pushed through by the U.S. Army Engineers in about eight months' time to get supplies and men to the Northland.

If you live in the Southwest or in the Pacific Coast states you can drive 1030 miles from Spokane, Washington, to Dawson Creek over the inland route via Calgary and Edmonton. Or you can start north from Seattle, drive the scenic Fraser River route in British Columbia, and span the new Hart Highway to Dawson Creek, a distance of 921 miles.

Whichever route you take, you'll find that driving to Dawson Creek is only the warm-up for your trip to Alaska.

The Alaska Highway from Dawson Creek to Fairbanks is 1520 miles, and from Dawson Creek to Anchorage is 1640 miles. You cannot drive to the Panhandle communities of Ketchikan, Petersburg, Juneau, Skagway or Sitka. They are not connected by highway with the Big Part of Alaska. The only Southeastern town that can be reached by the Alaska Highway is Haines, and it is accessible only through a branch road kept open during the summer. During that period ferry service connects Haines with the capital city of Juneau.

How many miles will you travel on a round trip from your home town back to your home town? By the time you have added about 1500 miles of sightseeing in Alaska, you will have chalked up a total of 7000 to 10,000 miles on your car. Considering that about 3000 miles of this is on gravel, it's obvious that this junket is not in the cards for the man on a two-weeks vacation.

The Alaska Highway is by no means a Pennsylvania Turnpike or a California Freeway, but it is a wide, well-maintained road. Twelve hundred twenty-one miles are in Canada, and most of this section is hard-packed crushed gravel. But blacktopping is starting to work its way northward from Dawson Creek.

By the time you read this, the last remaining section of the unpaved portion of the highway in Alaska will be blacktopped. After you have been eating dust and fighting fine gravel for more than a thousand miles, the blacktop will raise your morale more than a bottle of vitamin pills mixed with queen bee jelly.

The highway maintenance on both the Canadian and Alaskan sections of the highway is excellent. It would have to be, as regular trucking firms keep a four-day schedule between Seattle and Fairbanks and Seattle and Anchorage. The Minneapolis trucking schedule calls for delivery on the seventh day. These schedules are made possible by having two drivers on each truck, one hitting the sack over the cab while the other chews up the miles.

Despite the distance, many Alaskans prefer driving the highway to flying to and from the other states. After all, in an automobile you are not limited to sixty-six pounds of luggage — and you can take your time.

Many travelers come over the highway for these reasons alone. Fred and Sara Machetanz of High Ridge, near Palmer, made their first trip over the Alaska Highway ten years ago to lecture in the States. They needed their car to travel the lecture circuit and to carry their films and luggage.

This famous Alaskan artist-author-lecture team has now made twenty-one trips over the Alaska Highway. They graduated from a two-door to a station wagon when they started traveling with two beautiful husky dogs. "They're an important part of our TV and lecture shows," Sara explained, "and fortunately they are good travelers. But they are always so peppy when they get out of the car that we sometimes have to give them tranquilizers to get them to cooperate on the stage."

In ten years the Machetanzes have given more than six hundred lectures on Alaska throughout the United States and Canada. They have shot a hundred thousand feet of color film on the Northland, some of it for Walt Disney. Fred has painted portraits of Eskimos and captured the elusive beauty of the cold Arctic on canvas. Fred and Sara have written seven books on Alaska, one of which, *Rick of High Ridge,* is a juvenile fiction of a family driving to Alaska and homesteading in the Matanuska Valley.

The Machetanzes know the highway thoroughly. They have driven it in all seasons of the year and under all weather conditions.

"We camped out several trips to get the experience," Fred stated. "There are a sufficient number of public camp grounds on both sides of the border, with toilets and outdoor cooking facilities. If you have a lot of time — or a lot of children — that's a good way to travel. We found, though, that it takes about two hours a day longer to travel this way — setting up a tent, cooking, dishwashing, etc. It saves time to stop at roadhouses — but it's more expensive."

When the Machetanzes first drove the highway in the late 1940s its beauty was marred by more than a few hard realities — sharp rocks, blind turns, narrow curves and accommodations that were few and far between. They've seen the highway improved year after year until it is now considered the best graveled highway in the world. Some of the provincial roads of Canada, which lead to the Alaska Highway at Dawson Creek, have been transformed from virtually the worst in North America into paved thoroughfares. The oil derricks that dot the landscape throughout Alberta have been largely responsible for this improvement.

Accommodations have been upgraded, too. In the main they're clean, warm and sufficient to serve the needs of the traveler. "Of course, if you're looking for de luxe motels with TV, heated swimming pools, barbecue pits and dancing girl revues, we don't have them — yet," Fred said. "Right now, the highway roadhouses tend more to the 'bath is down the hall' variety.

"But even that's an improvement over a few years ago when most roadside stops were memorable for the 'Ladies' and 'Gents' out back — a never-to-be-forgotten experience during mosquito season or at twenty below."

Roadhouses, gas stations, cafes and motels dot the highway on an average of one for every thirty miles. Garages can handle both major and minor repairs and fix flats while you're having lunch. If you're camping out, there are plenty of places along the highway selling groceries, so it isn't necessary to load your car with staples.

Many of the roadhouse proprietors, out of necessity, are do-it-yourselfers. They are husband-and-wife owner-operators who have helped to build their own establishments, often cutting corners because they were undercapitalized. They do the cleaning, repairing and cooking — and that means being up half the night.

In spite of this, highway travelers remark on how friendly

and courteous the operators are — and how anxious they are to point out the attractions, scenery, wild game and good fishing spots. "The hospitality of these places more than makes up for what the accommodations may lack," Sara Machetanz pointed out.

How long does it take to drive to Alaska? That depends on how you drive. College boys have made it from Seattle to Fairbanks in three and a half days — driving fast around the clock, burning up the gravel, their tires and sometimes themselves. Highway patrolmen state that, next to excessive speed, most accidents on the Alaska Highway are caused by drowsy drivers and drivers falling asleep at the wheel.

"We've found that we can drive comfortably between three hundred and four hundred miles a day on the highway," Fred said. "The speed limit is posted for fifty mph, and if you have any respect for your tires — and for your life — you'll keep to it or under it. The faster you drive on a gravel road the hotter your tires get, and the danger of blowouts mounts with the heat. And when you come to a ridge of loose gravel, slow down!

"After all, the scenery on the Alaska Highway is magnificent, and you can't enjoy it if you're breaking all speed records," he continued. "If you want to get to Alaska in a hurry, take a plane.

"One thing you'll notice about the Alaska Highway is that a lot of the grades on hills go sharply up one side and down the other," Fred remarked. "When traffic is light most drivers steer smack down the center of the road, and this results in fatal head-on collisions two or three times a year. It's a good policy to keep to the right at all times — especially when you're coming up over a sharp rise or around a bad corner.

"In the summertime you have to watch out for those mammoth truck-and-trailer combinations, especially when it's dusty," he explained. "When you see one barreling down upon you, stirring up a junior-sized dust storm, get over to the side of the road, roll up your windows, turn on your lights and stop. If you don't stop, or at least slow down to a crawl, you'll find yourself in a cloud so thick you won't know which side of the road you're driving on. And after all, undertakers are a span apart on the Alaska Highway."

When is the best time to travel the highway?

As far as traffic is concerned, late April and early May are good months to come north, according to Fred. The days are getting longer then, too. This is the season of the breakup and trucks and vans are either under tonnage and speed limitations or they are not on the highway at all. The weight of the heavily loaded trucks, when the frost is oozing out of the ground, is plain dynamite to the roads. They break down the surface and a big maintenance job is the result. Passenger cars have an easy time of it because of lack of competition on the highway.

However, most travelers come over the highway in summer, because that is vacation time, or because they can camp out and the kids want to sleep in tents and cook food over open fires — just as the Hollywood Sourdoughs do on TV. But you will have to chase the junior-size explorers off to bed by the clock, because in June and July it doesn't get dark up here. If you come in summer, bring along several mosquito bombs and some bug lotion and be sure your tent is mosquito-proof.

In the summertime you'll find that your gas tank is especially exposed to road hazards, and many motorists have a garageman stretch a piece of rubber belting or inner tube against the underside of the tank as protection against punctures from flying gravel. If you are unlucky enough to get a leak, rub a bar of soap into the break, and that will keep you going until you reach a garage.

"If you can pick your time to travel to Alaska, the ideal scenic trip would be to come north in August, when the country is beautifully green and the fireweed and northern flowers are a riot of color," Fred advised. "Then head south in mid-September when the hillsides are splashed with fall colors and the sky is a vivid blue. The mosquitoes are gone at this season, and the air has a wonderful zip to it."

For the tourist, the scenery is spectacular any time of year. The Alaska Highway wanders through rolling farmland, green forests, beneath majestic mountains, alongside blue lakes and roaring rivers, skirts the historic Yukon — and goes through three time zones.

To make your trip more enjoyable, Fred recommends that you keep your color camera or your movie camera handy. "There are Indian families along the highway, and the chubby-cheeked children love to have their pictures taken. (They won't refuse a dime or a quarter, either.) Deer, moose, caribou, an occasional bear, birds and rabbits will pop out on the road or within photographing distance when you least expect them."

In the mountains you may see a convention of mountain goats or Dall sheep, and around Big Delta, about a hundred miles south of Fairbanks, there's a large herd of roaming buffalo that "own" all they survey in this part of Alaska. They'll lumber up on the highway, give you a glassy stare, and after you've run a hundred feet or so of film, and tooted your horn, they'll slowly move away.

The kiddies (and the grownups) will be disappointed that

they won't see Sergeant Preston — even in the Yukon. Unless you're in a Canadian town on the Queen's Birthday or an important provincial holiday you won't see any red-coated Royal Canadian Mounties at all. They'll be dressed in dark brown and will be seated behind the wheel of a patrol car — looking for all the world like any Stateside patrol officer who turns on his red flasher and gives you the siren — when you least expect it.

"Most Alaskans prefer driving the Alaska Highway in the winter when the ground is frozen solid and there is just enough snow on the road to cover the gravel and turn the highway into a white, paved boulevard," Fred stated. "No dust, no fuss, no heavy traffic. Also, there's no deep snow to worry about. The route of the highway is through the northern interior where precipitation is low.

"If you drive the highway in winter, have your car thoroughly winterized, check your defroster and put on snow tires," he went on. "Install a headbolt heater for cold morning starting, fill your radiator with anti-freeze down to sixty below, and have your thermostat set on 'high' so you'll get maximum heat in your car.

"Also — and this is very important — dress for cold weather. Too many statesiders driving north depend on car heat to keep them warm. Papa, get out your long johns — Mama, too," Fred cautioned. "Sara always wears wool slacks when we travel in winter.

"There isn't much traffic in the cold months, so you should be prepared for any reasonable emergency," Fred said. "Bring along sleeping bags and a day's food rations. When you start out each morning include a thermos of piping-hot coffee. Stow your tire chains, a shovel and a hundred feet of rope in the back of your car where you can get at them easily. And in winter, particularly, drive off the top half of your gas tank.

"Chances are you won't have to use any of your emergency gear," Fred said, "but if you slide off the road and have all this equipment you can probably get back on again yourself. Those truckers you cussed in summertime are a welcome sight in winter if you're stranded between roadhouses at fifty below. They'll always lend a helping hand."

The Alaska Highway patrol is authority for the statement that no one has frozen to death on any road in Alaska in the past six years. The highway is patrolled constantly both in Canada and Alaska, and though you may have to wait a while before someone comes along, if your car is warm and you're warm yourself you're in no danger.

The Machetanzes have driven the highway on a 10,000-mile round trip without engine trouble or without a blowout. Fred contends that most of the motor difficulties and tire troubles are caused by overloading the car and excessive speed.

"The fellow who goes ripping by me at seventy to eighty miles per hour, all loaded down, is flirting with the angels," he said. "Time and again Sara and I have made side bets on how soon we would see the character by the side of the road changing a tire or looking under the hood."

Half the fun of traveling to the 49th state is planning your trip, and there are several current publications which will give you excellent highway and roadside accommodation information.

One is *The Milepost,* the bible of northern travelry, which furnishes a mile-by-mile guide to everything on the Alaska Highway, the branch roads leading from the Alaska Highway, and the access roads traveling northward through Canada. *The Milepost* has been published since 1944 and is revised annually.

This publication contains all the information you should know about Canadian customs and regulations concerning firearms, dogs and cats traveling with you, automobile insurance, and bonding requirements in case you are towing a trailer or driving a car built prior to 1940.

With hundreds of house trailers being hauled to Alaska every year, Canadian customs has adopted a strict trailer code, specifying the size of car — and horsepower — required to pull trailers of various sizes.

Through sad experience Canada has played unwilling host to too many broken-down cars and abandoned trailers — all because the owner was attempting to pull a load too heavy for his underweight and underpowered vehicle.

Few drivers can stand the expense of having the rear end of their cars go out en route to Alaska, and that's what's happened to motorists when their trailers have been too heavy or their cars too loaded down. Besides towing charges to the nearest garage, parts may have to be flown or trucked in, and a week's delay can be prohibitively costly.

So if you're planning to haul a house trailer north with you, consult *The Milepost* before you leave. If your local newsdealer does not have this guidebook, write *The Milepost*, Box 2175, Anchorage, Alaska. The price is $1.35, air mail $1.75.

Another must for the highway traveler is the *Northwest Travelguide*, a fat, informative Canadian publication with special emphasis on all accommodations, attractions, villages and the numerous side roads of British Columbia. It also gives you a rundown on hunting and fishing spots, angling regulations and licenses, and camping facilities throughout

British Columbia and the Yukon. This excellent booklet is on sale at Alaska Highway newsstands, or may be ordered from *Northwest Travelguide*, Box 1238, Quesnel, B.C. The cost is $1.00, air mail $1.50.

Lou Jacobin's *Guide to Alaska* is an informative booklet listing Alaskan towns, their retail establishments and points of interest, and historical notes about the Northland. This book contains a wealth of information about the new state, and you can get it by writing to the Stateside distribution office at Box 856, Cathedral City, California, price $2.

These three publications, like all commercial guidebooks, depend on the advertising of lodges, stores, roadhouses and service industries for their revenue. Therefore, no attempt at grading the quality of each overnight stopping place and café is possible. You will have to evaluate these for yourself. Your job will be simplified, however, if you ask along the way for information regarding future stops.

Another mine of information is *A Guide to Resorts and Lodges* published by the British Columbia Government Tourist Bureau, Victoria, B.C. It does not carry advertising, and evaluates the quality of overnight accommodations and restaurants without fear or favor. This publication, which applies only to the province of British Columbia, is free for the asking.

How much does it cost to drive to Alaska? That depends on your appetite and the amount you want to spend — whether you dine on T-bone steaks or the blue-plate special, whether you camp out or stay at roadhouses, and whether your car is a foreign model that gets thirty-three miles to the gallon or a fintailed giant that gets you all of fifteen. Also whether or not you can resist the blandishments of the ever-present Alaskan curios and native souvenirs.

On the basis of averaging 300 to 400 miles of driving per day from Great Falls or Seattle to Fairbanks or Anchorage, the trip will take you from seven to eight days. Meals for two adults will average about $85, lodging $80, gas and oil $85 — a total of about $250.

But don't start out on an economy budget. If you have a blowout and have to buy a new tire, or have car trouble, your cash funds will disappear very rapidly.

Be sure to talk with your insurance agent before you start north. Many automobile insurance policies require a special endorsement to cover you in Yukon Territory.

Before you leave home consult your local gas station as to whether or not your credit card is acceptable in Canada and Alaska. Standard Oil of California and Union Oil Company practically blanket the north country. If you have these credit cards your gas tank need never be empty. Incidentally, both these companies distribute free excellent up-to-date maps of the Alaska Highway and the state of Alaska.

If you decide to drive to Alaska, start out with good tires. If your car comes equipped with tubeless tires, bring along a couple of tubes to fit. Should you have punctures and cannot get your tubeless tire fixed immediately, the tubes will put you back on the road. Buy live rubber tubes, not synthetics. The latter tend to crack in cold weather.

A word about hitchhikers on the Alaska Highway — *let them hike!*

Hitchhiking in the Northland is increasing every season, and the highway patrol warns that you invite either men or women thumbers into your car at your own risk.

"It's one thing to pick up a driver who's run out of gas and give him a lift to the next garage, but it's something else again to pick up the 'professional' hitchhiker who knows his rights," a patrolman said. "He can claim he's been injured in your car, and you'll be paying him damages the rest of your life."

If you're driving north over the highway, the United States Immigration Service at Tok Junction will ask if you've picked up any hitchhikers. If you have one riding with you, and if he turns out to be an inadmissable alien, you will have to return him to the Canadian immigration service — one hundred twelve miles back down the road.

United States citizens passing through Canada to Alaska do not need passports, but it's a good idea to have proper identification with you. Naturalized citizens should carry a special card of identification.

"Just one further thought I'd like to pass on," Fred Machetanz said. "On our lecture tours we are approached by people planning to drive to Alaska and to pay for their trips by selling their cars in Anchorage or Fairbanks at a handsome profit.

"It can't be done. Alaska is loaded with used-car lots and glutted with cars for sale. The cash offer you will get for your car will put your heart in your boots," he said.

"After all, a model fresh from the factory has a lot of rough miles on it after it has been over the Alaska Highway, and from a buyer's viewpoint, is a long way from being a new car.

"My suggestion is, forget about selling your car and enjoy your trip to Alaska. It will be a wonderful experience you will talk about for the rest of your life — or until you decide to drive to Alaska again."

Book Two

7

Want a Job in Alaska?

JUST ABOUT EVERY DAY OF THE WEEK AN OFFICE of the Alaska State Employment Service gets a long-distance call from somebody in Florida, California, Connecticut or Texas who has decided to come north and prosper in Alaska — the land of opportunity.

To many, the words "job" and "opportunity" are synonymous with Alaska. The Northland has a magical meaning. Anyone can go to Alaska and get any kind of job and make his fortune. You don't need any particular know-how or experience — you just "go North, young man."

Maybe you'll go up and do a little fishing — after all, Alaska's waters produce $70,000,000 in fish every year. Or maybe you'll mine gold, or work on one of those fabulous missile projects. What matter that you have been a boomer — or that you haven't had enough training in any particular trade or profession to qualify for a steady job.

The idea, concocted from fantastic stories in newspapers and magazines, and mixed with a little wishful thinking, seems to be if you can get to Alaska you've got it made. If you're a bank clerk it won't take long to become a business tycoon. And if you're a counter girl in the five-and-ten you can strike it rich at a military base. Some of those who phone from the other states say "Alaska here I come!" — and expect a job on arrival.

"Some of these phone calls run to thirty and forty dollars," said Morris Schrock, manager of the Anchorage office of the Alaska State Employment Service. "Each caller is so certain that he can make a barrel of money in Alaska that he is reluctant to listen to the facts of life, even though he is paying for the call and wants information. As soon as I get a word in edgewise, I ask right away about his trade or profession and his job history.

"You'd be surprised, but the majority of the calls are from construction workers and from men and women who have factory skills or have a long-time experience on an assembly line," Schrock said. "They want a change of scenery, and some of that high Alaskan pay they've been reading about, so they decide to screw on bolts in a factory in Alaska instead of in a factory on Long Island.

"It sometimes takes quite a while to get it across to them that there is no such thing as a factory job in Alaska, because there are no factories up here," Schrock said. "I've been called untruthful because I said we didn't have any assembly plants to build tractors, refrigerators, washing machines, watches or anything else up here. People who have never been outside of a crowded manufacturing community find it virtually impossible to accept life without an assembly line.

"I explain that the 49th state is still in the primary stage of development — meaning that it's still just a producer of raw materials. There is no place as yet in our economy for the skilled factory worker who is the backbone of our eastern manufacturing states."

A lot of three-day wonders who become authorities on

Alaska after a rocket-ride through the new state write stories about the fabulous wages paid carpenters, plumbers, heavy-duty operators and truck drivers. As a result, every spring hundreds of workers fly north with the first honkers, their hopes pinned on enough overtime to put them in the big money league.

What these writers fail to point out is that, though a plumber's paycheck may be double what he receives in the other states, so are his living costs. And most of the fantastic reports of high wages are holdovers from the war construction era, with its cost-plus jobs and all the overtime a man could physically absorb.

In those days Alaska did not have a resident labor supply. Thousands of men were recruited from the States to construct military establishments needed in a hurry. But with the doubling of Alaska's population in the past ten years, the residents of the new state are more than filling the construction needs.

"Today Alaska has more laborers, carpenters, plumbers, heavy-duty operators and truck drivers looking for work than all the missile sites, radar installations and civilian construction can absorb," Schrock stated. "In fact, *unemployment in these trades is higher in Alaska than in any other state in the Union.*

"I always tell a tradesman that if he has a reasonably good job, satisfactory working conditions and a happy home, he'd better stay where he is instead of selling everything and taking a chance on Alaska," Schrock said. "If he has enough money for a vacation trip, I suggest that he come up and see for himself what conditions are like. In most cases, a trip would convince him.

"Just because you hear that they're building a new fifty-million-dollar pulp mill in Southeastern Alaska, or that half a billion has been appropriated for new missile anti-missile sites in the Arctic, it doesn't mean that they're hiring hundreds of workers," Schrock went on. "In every call for tradesmen to go out on the job there are more than enough Alaskans waiting to fill it."

Because of the short summer season, five to seven months is the maximum time you can expect to be hired on an outdoor construction job. The same thing holds true in the mining industry. With high production costs, mining in Alaska today is at a low ebb and employs few workers.

In the fishing industry, more automation in the canneries, and periodically curtailed fishing seasons to protect the salmon runs from extinction, have taken their toll of employees. Trollers are usually one-man boats, and seiners have only two to four men. Most of the larger fishing vessels pick up their crews in Seattle and go back to fish along the Pacific Coast or South America after the Alaska season is over. Workers for the salmon canneries are generally imported from Seattle, Bellingham and San Francisco for the short canning season, and there is little opportunity for inexperienced workers in the fishing industry.

Alaska's logging industry, too, is a seasonal operation and pulp mills have a backlog of available personnel.

Then how do you go about getting a job in Alaska?

Not by rushing north and hammering on the door of the Alaska employment offices. Nor by cornering a prospective employer in Fairbanks or Nome.

"We would like to impress upon people that they should get their jobs *before* they come to Alaska," Schrock said. "Or if they come to Alaska without any prospects, they must have sufficient funds to tide them over for possibly several months until something turns up or they decide to return home. Right now we've got people arriving here with nothing to do except swell the rolls of the unemployed.

"To find out what jobs are available in Alaska, all you have to do is go to your nearest state employment office and ask to see the current 'Bulletin on Job Opportunities in Alaska,'" Schrock went on. "The Alaska State Employment Service, which has offices in Fairbanks, Anchorage, Homer, Juneau, Petersburg and Ketchikan, is part of the federal Employment Service, and current employment bulletins are sent from Alaska to each of the other states. If your local office doesn't have the most recent bulletin, it can get a copy from your state headquarters.

"If you see something that interests you, the local office will take your qualifications and job history and forward them by air mail to the Alaskan office," Schrock stated. "You will hear direct from the prospective employer and you can handle your own negotiations from there on in. There is no charge for job placement by the Alaska State Employment Service."

Government employment, most of it through civil service, accounts for about 40 per cent of the labor force of Alaska. If you're a civil service career employee, with an itchy foot and a desire to see Alaska, you have a better than average chance of getting a job in the 49th state. The biggest employers are the Federal Aviation Agency, the Department of the Interior, the Weather Bureau, Post Office, Department of Health, Education and Welfare and the Department of Defense. Your nearest Civil Service Commission office will have a list of federal job openings in Alaska. Generally speaking, the job descriptions and working conditions in federal employment are the same in Alaska as in the other states. As in other communities, federal employees have their own credit unions and their own social organizations.

At the present time, all federal employees enjoy a 25 per cent cost-of-living differential over other state federal employees to help compensate for the higher cost of living in Alaska. In fact, wages for any job are usually higher in Alaska than they are in the other states, but living costs tend to eat up the differential.

Alaska has a number of privately owned employment agencies, but in most cases they handle the same listings as does the State Employment Service. Most privately operated agencies charge you 40 per cent of your first month's wages for placing you in a job.

It is not necessary to pay for information concerning jobs or possible jobs in Alaska. Nor is it necessary to buy advertised lists of contractors or detailed contract awards. The State Employment Service has all job information free. Under no circumstances should you pay for any job *before* you get it.

Thousands of trusting souls throughout the United States have parted with their hard-earned cash in answer to advertisements like the following:

JOBS IN ALASKA

Openings for all crafts and unskilled labor now available in the 49th state. High pay, lots of overtime. We are a screening service for many contractors on missile sites, defense construction, etc. Fill out the coupon below, attach a $20 bill, and we will notify you by return mail when personnel interviewer will contact you. Be prepared to leave for Alaska in 30 days or less. Make this your year for big money in Alaska. Send your letter air mail to our Alaskan office.

The —— Company
Anchorage, Alaska

One ad alone which appeared in a number of big-city newspapers pulled six thousand letters, and the easy take would have been $120,000 if the authorities had not stepped in. The jobs, of course, were nonexistent. No reputable contractor ever charges for job information or for job offers.

Unfortunately this type of bunko game is on the increase. For a "fee" some of the nefarious operators offer "specific" jobs in Fairbanks or Anchorage, and these operators are causing untold misery and hardships. Numerous families are arriving in the Northland to start work on jobs which don't exist.

A man, wife and three school-age children drove into Fairbanks on a freezing morning in November to accept one of these phony jobs. They had sold everything they owned in Cleveland and had driven up over the Alaska Highway in an old car. They counted out $35.11 among the five of them when they found they had come on a wild goose chase of over four thousand miles.

It is heartbreaking to see people like this comb the town — first to find the nonexistent job, and then to try to locate the guy who swindled them. The Salvation Army usually gets these cases on its hands, and tries to get the hungry, badly disillusioned families back to their homes in the other states.

What happened to the fast-buck operator? He's long since departed for warmer climes. The usual routine is to hire a post office box in an Alaskan town, then supply the postmaster with a forwarding address to some big city Outside. A confederate picks up the letters and money at the big city general delivery window. Sometimes he is met at the window by the postal authorities and the jig is up. But in other cases he manages to keep just one post office ahead of the law.

Alaska has received so much publicity since statehood that the state employment offices are deluged with correspondence from people who would like to start fresh in the new state. The letters come from all the other states, from Europe, from Africa and from Australia.

"We get all kinds of letters," Schrock said, "literate, incoherent, humorous and pathetic. Many of the writers are inexperienced and are not prepared financially to come to Alaska. Here's a note the Chamber of Commerce received the other day:

" 'Dear Sir: We want to move to Alaska. It sounds like the land of opertunity for a young couple. How about jobs? My wife is pregnunt. Is it alright for her to come up now? We'd like this information as soon as possible. E.B.'

"You'll notice the writer doesn't say what he can do — or what his trade is. Chances are he's very young, just out of high school, and recently married. Alaska is an expensive place to learn any job, and unless this couple has adequate financing they had better make their stake first and then come north."

To answer the thousands of inquiries put to them about working possibilities in Alaska, the Alaska Employment Service sends out an eighteen-page booklet entitled *Alaska Job Facts*. This booklet not only explains in detail the character of the Alaska labor market, but it gives a picture of living conditions and living costs in the various communities and tells how to go about getting a job in the new state.

Alaska Job Facts spells out one of the important factors in going to work in Alaska: every trade, every craft, and several of the professions in the Northland have their own unions. One paragraph states:

"The construction industry is highly unionized, and employment is governed by collective bargaining agreements and hiring practices. In addition, preference is ordinarily given to the resident worker. Therefore, the construction job seeker who comes to Alaska without any job offer may have a long wait before he finds the job for which he is qualified and in which he is interested."

In simple language, that means you must be a union member if you expect to remain employed on a construction job. If you are a member of a union in another state, you must have a Travel Card to get on the list up here. All unions recognize and accept the Travel Card, but it gives you no preference for employment. Your name goes on the bottom of the list, and you have to wait your turn to be called for a job.

It is entirely likely that a recent NLRB statement of policy may be put into effect shortly in Alaska. That pronouncement will require a year of residence in any locale before your name will be added to the list of persons available for employment. And few persons can afford to sit around unemployed anywhere in Alaska for a year.

The NLRB may enforce this as a protection to local residents who, in all the other states, are given preference in employment before persons from outside the state are hired. The Board feels that such a policy would tend to stabilize the labor market in Alaska where there have been so much seasonal work and so many transient laborers.

There is another phase to employment in Alaska which you should consider. If you come north with a large family, you won't be able to send your children out to bring in the beans and bacon. The Alaska Child Labor Law permits only baby sitting or casual employment like newspaper selling and delivery, and no juvenile under eighteen may operate a commercial motor vehicle or ride as a helper-employee. So you will have to be employed yourself if you want to keep the family in warm clothes.

So far in this chapter we have talked about the laborer, the semiskilled worker and the construction worker who are going to find it tough to locate a job in the new state because of the surplus of able-bodied men and women now living in Alaska. Also the factory worker for whom there is no demand, as Alaska does not have a manufacturing industry.

But lest any reader feel we are backtracking on our theme that Alaska is the promised land for the right kind of people, let us state that there *are* numerous job openings throughout Alaska. Every morning the local radio stations in all Alaskan towns read off lists of job vacancies. They run something like this:

Top-grade stenographers, secretaries, nurses, insurance adjusters, psychiatric social workers, electronics technicians and engineers, draftsmen, IBM operators and marine engineers — experienced personnel only.

Today there is need throughout the 49th state for the well-trained white collar worker and the professional man or woman — doctors, dentists, medical technicians and teachers. To get in touch with one of these openings, a professional man or woman fills out a special managerial and professional application form at his local employment office and specifies he's interested in Alaska. The form is air-mailed to the Anchorage Employment Office which is the "network center" for all applications and openings for professional employment.

Personnel assigned to this specialized work have earned the confidence of local employers and often get positions opened up earlier than normal in order to make use of a highly qualified applicant.

"We are very anxious to encourage persons with professional skills and unusual training to come north," Schrock stated. "Frequently we are successful in promoting jobs for specially qualified men or women. When that happens we're always gratified to see them become useful citizens in the new state."

The need for professional people varies from town to town, and this is the reason we stress one fact strongly: come up and see *all* of Alaska before you decide whether or not to settle here.

Doctors tend to gravitate to the larger towns because of the greater populations and better hospital facilities. The young doctor just getting started may find it more lucrative to settle in one of the smaller communities. The same goes for dentists and attorneys. There are lawyers in every town, and some cities have a surplus, but if you're a good attorney, and are willing to work, you can make a fortune up here. Alaska has reciprocity with certain states, otherwise attorneys must pass the Alaska Bar examination. Doctors, dentists, and chiropractors must also pass a state board examination.

The turnover in many white collar jobs such as accountants and bank personnel is greater in Alaska than in many places Outside. If a man is competent and a good worker he often gets a better offer from another firm or in another town, or he decides he wants to return to the other states. Those who stick with their jobs find they have a better chance of quick promotion than they would elsewhere. Alaska has several bank vice-presidents in their late thirties and early forties who would still be assistant tellers if they'd stayed in their home towns.

Schrock turned to his desk. "Even though Alaska is the flyingest state in the Union, the only fliers Alaska needs right now are helicopter pilots with two thousand hours of passenger flying. I can show you thirty applications on hand from multi-engine pilots — they can fly practically anything. But at present Alaska has an oversupply of fly-boys. Airlines up here follow the seniority rule and make promotions from within the ranks. Too, a newcomer would have a hard time competing with the experienced bush pilot who not only knows the terrain and weather conditions, but knows how to take care of himself in the wilds of the Northland.

"We also have a surplus of airplane mechanics, as well as garage mechanics, although there is frequently an opportunity for these crafts if a man will take a job in a small community or a bush village," Schrock said. "Most mechanics want to stick around the bigger towns."

As far as the "arts" are concerned, Alaska is very culturally minded, but you can count on your fingers the number of people who are making a living teaching music and dancing. The mortality rate on music and dancing academies has been high because of the small population; however a number of married women have made a nice little nest egg with part-time music and dancing pupils. If you plan to come up and make your living as a journalist, the Employment Service is the authority that good reporters are now acting as soda-jerks, hoping for an opening on one of the state's news-papers.

As the total population of Alaska is only 225,000, the retail sales market in the new state is relatively small. Alaska has no large department stores as we know them in the other states. The Northern Commercial Company's store in An-chorage is the largest department store north of Edmonton, and it employs an average of a hundred and twenty persons. The N.C. Company also has department stores in Fairbanks and Nome and in Whitehorse, Yukon Territory, and trading posts in small communities throughout Alaska.

Specialty shops, drugstores and supermarkets in Alaskan towns hire from three to twenty-five persons, and clerks are cleared through the Retail Clerks Union. Although Alaska has more than its share of bars and cocktail establishments, the bar business is 100 per cent unionized and operates in a tight circle.

Because business establishments are small — many of them family operations — Alaska cannot yet absorb young executives of the "gray flannel suit" variety. A company's young executive is also apt to be its salesman and its janitor. And those who are in line for top positions in the few larger establishments have usually learned the business from the ground up.

Jack Ferguson spent twelve years at Northern Commercial Company trading posts out in the bush before he became general manager of the company's Anchorage operations. "We did every conceivable job — stoked fires, hauled ice, checked cargo, repaired outboard motors, doctored sick sled dogs, waited on the trade — even to all-day suckers for the children," Jack related. "When we were promoted to the McGrath store we finally got a flush toilet — the only one in the whole Kuskokwim River area at that time. It was the showpiece of a hundred thousand square miles.

"We've had our share of applications from young executives who have somewhere picked up the misconception that if they're willing to come to Alaska they can start at the top," Jack said. "One young fellow flew up here from the East Coast to look over business possibilities. He was under thirty, had two degrees from one of the larger Eastern universities, and made no bones about the fact that he was looking for an executive position with an executive's salary.

"Somewhere he'd read about the opportunities in the great Northland, and felt there was no need for starting at the bottom and working up — not in Alaska.

"Even though he may be an excellent administrator, he still has a lot to learn about the psychology of the north country and the people," Jack said. "You just don't do business in Alaska the way you do in the other states."

In every town located near a defense base there is a large readymade market of wives and dependents of military personnel. These persons are employed as teachers, hospital aides, salespeople — in almost every category of job available in the Northland. And when these dependents rotate, there are always new ones to take their places.

Generally speaking, job opportunities will be occurring in those service industries and professions which increase in size and grow in number with an expanding population. Alaska's population may well be 1,000,000 in the next twenty years. That means we'll need not only more white collar workers, but more service industry employees and more homes for our population.

But don't rush north on the strength of what might happen within the next twenty years. As one official in the Employment Service said, "Alaska has gobs of potential, but our clients want jobs for their immediate bread and butter. Plenty of Alaskans find it hard to get jobs to keep them going from day to day."

Despite its reams of publicity, Alaska's oil industry is one of the businesses still strictly in its potential. Oil companies are importing what personnel they need for this technical work.

If you accept a job or position in Alaska, and you haven't been up here before, Schrock suggests that you first fly up here *alone*. Find out for yourself if Alaska is the glamor land you hope it will be. Perhaps your job, as far as you are concerned, will turn out to be a "lousy deal"; the working conditions may not be to your liking or the small town not to your fancy. Or perhaps if you get a job in Central or Northwest Alaska you'll be allergic to wearing long johns six months out of the year.

Then you'll be awfully glad you didn't move your family up. You can just pack your suitcase, wipe the mud, dust or snow from your shoes, get aboard an airplane and, as one worker said, "give the goddam country back to the Eskimos."

Obviously the jobs we have been discussing so far do not in any way include the opportunities you create for yourself. If you have enough capital to put yourself into business up here — into the business in which you are highly skilled or trained by profession — then your success or failure depends strictly on yourself.

If you want to get into business for yourself, you should have about three times as much cash and credit to start in Alaska as you would need in one of the other states.

Before you decide where to locate, make a reconnaissance trip to Alaska and take enough time and enough money to study all of the state at first hand. If there normally would be a chance for you to practice your profession or training in a community of three thousand persons, plan your itinerary to cover every community of three thousand or more in the new state.

Get acquainted with the mayor, the newspaper editor, the minister of your denomination, the school board, the manager of the Chamber of Commerce, the service clubs and women's organizations. If they feel that you are really interested, they'll take all the time you want to give you a correct picture of the community — its social aspects, its psychology and its trading possibilities.

If you feel that you will fit into the life of the community then say a few nice things about your wonderful family and the grand gal who is the mainspring of your existence. A few sincere remarks about your wife will do a lot to help her get adjusted in the community when she and the youngsters arrive.

But don't jump to conclusions about Alaska — particularly the smaller communities. Take a cold, hard look at yourself and your family as members of each community. Is your wife the type who can readily adjust to the small town? Does she enjoy the women's clubs, church work, PTA and the garden club?

If she dislikes community activities and simply cannot be happy in a small, self-contained town, then no matter how much money you can make, it isn't worth it.

But if you and your family can make yourselves a part of the Alaskan community you choose, and you have the personality to make your services in demand, then you'll like Alaska. You'll work hard, but you'll be one of those fortunate persons who makes his fortune in the great new state.

It takes very little to trigger off a new deluge of job-seeking pen pals from all parts of the globe. When an Anchorage newspaper publisher gave a speech in Dallas, Texas, on Alaska's oil development, he spotted some attractive young ladies in the audience and quipped that they should come up to Alaska to get husbands. Though women exceed men in the other states, he said, there are sixteen males for every ten females in Alaska.

The wire services left the publisher's oil remarks strictly alone, but they teletyped his "sixteen males to every ten females" around the world. Letters came by air mail from as far away as Australia wanting to know what kind of job a girl could get while picking out a husband in Alaska.

A million Americans would love to come to Alaska right now if they could land jobs up here. The Department of the Interior alone receives about two thousand letters a week asking for information on Alaska. And if you counted up all the inquiries received by Chambers of Commerce and other organizations you'd find they run over ten thousand per month.

"We do not want to discourage people from coming to Alaska, but we are highly concerned with labor coming into a market that is already top-heavy in many trades," Schrock summarized.

"In Alaska, professionally trained young people with proper financing have a better chance for success than they would have in the older states. With Alaska's rapid growth, these people can prosper with Alaska's development."

Schrock turned to his files. "So far we haven't had a long-distance call from New Guinea," he remarked with a smile, "but there is a first time for everything.

"Excuse me while I answer the telephone."

8

160 Acres Free

IF YOU FEEL IT IN YOUR BONES THAT YOU WANT to homestead in Alaska, then draw up a chair. After all, free land is still about 90 per cent of the urge for the Northland, and Alaska is practically the only remaining spot under the American flag where there are any large quantities of free land left.

This chapter will give you all the essential information you will need for the mechanics of filing on your 160 acres. But it won't supply you with the backbone and intestinal fortitude to go through with the hard job of proving up on your future home. Nor will it tell you how to go about cultivating your land if you don't know a plow from a potato masher.

Lest you get discouraged, let us say right here that hundreds of Americans, no better endowed than you, have successfully carried through with Uncle Sam's requirements, and now own 160 acres free and clear in Alaska.

We have discussed the whole homesteading procedure with Irving Anderson, the capable and cooperative manager of the Anchorage Land Office, and with Dale Zimmerman, the chief adjudicator for this area, who knows all the fine legal aspects of homesteading. The Anchorage office is the largest in the state, handling over 75 per cent of the home-stead filings, and the staff of this office has been through just about every human situation which could arise in connection with acquiring land from Uncle.

"Three-fourths of the people want to know how to home-stead in a hurry," Anderson stated. "But there is no such thing. You can't cut corners where Uncle Sam is concerned. The government lists specific requirements for residence and land improvements, and you have to comply with *all* of them before you can get a patent.

"We also have to inform the public that the U.S. Government Land Office is not a real estate agency," he went on. "People come in clamoring to buy 160 acres of good home-stead land outright. They've got to have it in a hurry. But we tell them no soap. After all, being able to homestead in Alaska is one of the things that makes this country a land of opportunity."

Land-hungry hopefuls from all over the old 48 states are now migrating north. If you're one of them, the land office has a preliminary word of advice. Before you grab at the first piece of open land you see, tour all the sections of the new state which have any agricultural possibilities, and then make up your mind where you want to settle. After all, Alaska is more than ten times the size of Iowa, and in such a vast area there are several types of climate, and as many varieties of soil and crop possibilities. These agricultural vital statistics are described in the chapter "The Straight Dope on Agriculture."

When you decide what general area you'd like to home-stead in, then you check in with the land office in that jurisdiction. There are three land offices in Alaska. The Juneau office covers the Panhandle. The Anchorage office controls everything from Mt. Fairweather, below Yakutat, westward to the end of the Aleutian Chain and northward to the summit of the Alaska Range. The Fairbanks office has supervision of all land north and west of the Alaska Range.

Let's assume you've decided to homestead in Southcentral Alaska. This is Mr. Anderson's bailiwick, so you head for the land office in Anchorage. You park your car in front of the building on East Fifth Avenue, put a nickel in the parking meter, take a numbered ticket at the door of the office, and join the other land-hopefuls in the waiting room. Chances are there'll be anywhere from five to twenty persons looking at maps, making out forms and talking with the clerks behind the counter, so you'll have to wait until your number comes up.

When your turn arrives, you'll find yourself talking to an efficient lady clerk who speaks in aliquot descriptions and knows most of the answers to homestead problems. (An aliquot description is the way homestead surveyors describe a piece of land; i.e. the NW¼ of Sec. 6, T 3 N, R 4 W, Seward Meridian.)

If you're smart you'll lay your cards on the table with this little lady right away — "I'd like to find out about homesteading. I don't have the faintest idea how to go about it, or where to choose my land. What do I do first?" — and you'll get her sympathetic help and undivided attention.

First she'll give you a booklet entitled *Information Bulletin No. 2 on Alaska* which contains the latest technical data on homesteading and can be readily understood by anyone who has had an elementary education. Then she'll lay out large maps showing general areas open for homesteading in the Southcentral district.

"You'll have to make up your own mind which area you want to file in," she explains. "These maps show the surveyed land open in the Kenai, the Matanuska Valley, the Susitna Basin, the Copper River Valley and other sections. If you haven't already been to these areas, I'd advise you to look over each one carefully before you decide where to tie yourself down.

"This will take time, but it's the only way you can be sure you've found the best spot," she points out. "And you can't tell what the soil is like from the color on the map, or viewing it through a foot of snow. Sourdoughs will tell you the best time to pick out acreage is in the fall, when you can see what nature produces on the land; how much of the acreage is swampy, how much is high ground, and how much is natural pasture.

"Talk with the homesteaders in the area and find out how they're getting along. That way you'll get some idea of whether the land is as good as you hope it is."

She's not required to give you any advice, but if she feels you're sincerely interested in getting a homestead, she'll probably give you the benefit of her experience in the land office.

"Here are a few things to consider," she'll say. "Your acreage may not be on a road, but a mile or two back in the bush. Do you really want to get way out there? What about the kids going to school? How will your wife like it out there? It can get awfully lonesome in the wintertime."

After touring all the areas, and weighing all the pros and cons of each one, let's say you've settled on a piece of land that's open for homesteading and looks just like your dream of heaven on earth. The law says you must walk over the

land and personally examine each of the four 40-acre sub-
divisions and measure it out from a U.S. survey marker in
the area.

After you've done that, you can hop in your jalopy, drive
one hundred miles back to the land office, and fill out your
"Application for Homestead Entry."

On this form you certify you are a United States citizen
twenty-one years of age — or, if younger, that you are head
of a family. You declare that you do not own as much as
160 acres in the United States — because the theory of
homesteading is to get land into the hands of the have-nots.
(The law being what it is, however, you can own 159 acres
in the other states that you've acquired by homestead, purchase, gift or inheritance — and still homestead 160 acres in
Alaska.)

Then you fill out the proper aliquot description of the
land you're applying for, pay the land office $16, and go back
to your quarters and wait for the clerks to catch up with all
the applications ahead of yours. The land office is swamped,
but the staff will process your form just as quickly as possible.

Sometimes it turns out that the land you have chosen has
been recently appropriated for government use, such as a
military withdrawal, FAA navigation site, game refuge or
moose reserve. If this turns out to be the case, you'll have to
choose another 160 acres. You can get awfully mad about
this, but it won't do you a bit of good.

If the U.S. Geological Survey states that your 160-acre
tract has been classified as mineral land, or that it has possibilities of oil and gas, or coal, you can still have the land
if you want it, but you'll have to sign a waiver reserving to
Uncle Sam all subsurface rights. If the land turns out to be

oil land, and produces a million barrels, you're merely a spectator. None of it belongs to you.

If the land is within a hundred miles or so of Anchorage, chances are good that some company has already leased the oil and gas rights from Uncle Sam for 50 cents per acre. If no one has, and if you want both the surface rights to your land and what's down below, you can lease the oil rights separately for 50 cents an acre (with a 640-acre minimum for the oil).

But if you have any kind of money to throw into the wildest speculation under the 49th flag, you'd better ask yourself what in the world are you doing homesteading in Alaska.

Let's assume that your land was not appropriated for some other use, and was not classified as mineral or oil and gas land.

As soon as your application is processed, you'll receive a "Notice of Allowance" from the land office. This means you may move onto the land and pitch your tent or build a cabin or haul in a trailer home. Actually you have six months before you must officially start your residence on your 160 acres, but if you're like most homesteaders you'll move right in and start to prove up so that you can claim the land in a minimum of three years.

During these three years you must live on the land seven months out of each year. You must cultivate at least $\frac{1}{16}$ of the acreage in the second year, and $\frac{1}{8}$ in the third year. This means that you must have cleared at least twenty acres, broken the sod, tilled the soil and planted a crop. The crop is usually brome grass for hay, or peas and oats, or vetch and oats, or potatoes.

One of the quirks of the law is that you must cultivate

the acreage, but you don't have to harvest the crops.

"Clearing a homestead is expensive," a Kenai farmer told us, with a few choice words thrown in. "To get anywhere and meet your requirements you gotta hire a bulldozer to clear the trees and brush. You gotta get a gang plow to turn the soil, and then a fleet of harrows to chew it up. You gotta do this *if* you're going to do any genuine farming.

"But if you just want to do the minimum work to prove up on your place, you can cut out some of the work after the bulldozers have stripped the trees and brush off. Lots of fellows who never intend to farm hand-sow their brome grass or oats and vetch.

"But by the time you have bulldozed a road into your homestead, put up a house or log cabin for the family, cleared land and planted a crop, you'll say 'free' land? Hell. You gotta have a fat backlog and a steady job if you're going to last out three years. I can tell you that from my own experience.

"Being out here in the bush is tough on the wife, too," he explained. "She gets sick with loneliness and has a bad case of cabin fever from being cooped up all winter with small kids and no place to go or no one else to talk to."

Along with isolation, primitive living conditions are more than some wives can put up with. One couple we know built a large log home on their homestead, every bit with their own hands. It had a nice view of a lake and some comfortable furniture, but in the kitchen was an old-fashioned wood range and a leaky hand pump. The privy was out in the back. "When REA comes, things'll be different," the wife promised herself.

But when REA arrived, the husband was so used to the status quo that he refused to put in anything but electric lights. He sank their savings into a new root cellar and went on pumping water by hand. He could never understand why his wife went Outside and has never returned.

Another quirk in the homestead law permits you to live in a tent or a trailer all during your homesteading days, but before you submit "Final Proof" for your homestead you must have a habitable house on the acreage. If you are single, this can be an eight by ten-foot one-room cabin, sufficiently insulated so you can live in it the year round.

Although it isn't cricket, it isn't against the law to haul in a house to meet the "habitable" qualification just before you're ready to prove up.

Incidentally, a habitable house does not mean electric lights and running water. But as one farm wife said, "Thank heavens REA finally got off the main highways and is reaching out to us in the bush. You can stand just about anything on a homestead if you have electricity."

When your three years are up (Uncle Sam allows you up to five years if you need it), you submit your Final Proof. You attest that you have complied with all the provisions of the law. So do two witnesses who swear they know you, know your land, and know that you have obeyed the residence and cultivation requirements. You state that you have not sold, bartered, given away, optioned, mortgaged, or agreed to option or mortgage or sell or give away even one foot of the homestead. If Uncle Sam finds you have been guilty of any one of these things, you'll get booted off the land.

If your Final Proof is approved, you dig down in your jeans and come up with $12.80 to cover clerical work. Years ago the government figured it cost exactly $12.80 to perform this service, and through the years the law has never been changed. Today it costs many times that figure, but you still pay $12.80.

A representative of the Bureau of Land Management then visits your homestead and measures the exact acreage you have under cultivation. He determines what land improvements you have made, takes a picture of your house, and talks with your neighbors and others in the vicinity — even the tavern keeper — to be sure you've complied with residence requirements and other qualifications.

If everything is found to be in proper order, you publish notice of proof in a newspaper for five consecutive weeks — and pay for the same. This five-week period gives anyone an opportunity to contest your claim to the land — to say that you didn't live there seven months out of the year, or that you made a secret deal to sell part of it, and so on. If there is no contest, or if a contest turns out to be false, then you may expect your patent in a month or two. This impressive document will arrive by certified mail from Washington, D. C., after being duly signed by the Chief of the Patent Section of the Bureau of Land Management.

And once you have this fancy-looking certificate in your hands you may do anything with the land you care to. But don't pull the cork out of the bottle until you've registered the patent with the recorder in your district and the State Land Office in Anchorage. Then in case anything happens to your certificate, you won't be tied up in Washington red tape to prove your title to the land.

If you're a veteran — male or female — of World War II or the Korean campaign, with nineteen months or more of service to your credit, Uncle Sam lops off some of the residence and time requirements for your homestead.

You must live on your 160 acres seven months of the first year *only*, but you must have a habitable house and have ⅛ of your acreage under cultivation before you can get your patent at the end of the third year.

Prior to the Act of 1954, a veteran could get a homestead merely by living on the land for seven months and building a habitable house. At the end of about a year, Uncle Sam gave him title to the land.

This resulted in thousands of acres of good land — especially in the fertile Kenai area where the Russians farmed in the 1800s — being taken up by veterans. After the vets got their patents, fully 90 per cent of them hightailed it Outside, and nobody knows where to reach them. This land is out of circulation, and it may be years before proper use can be made of the acreage.

One of the field examiners still shakes his head over what he calls the "habitable house racket." After examining several vets' applications over a period of several months, and checking their homesteads, he found that all the "habitable houses" looked suspiciously alike. Upon further examination it turned out that the boys were moving the house from one homestead to another as the seven months' period was up and the examiner was due to arrive.

If you're a veteran of World War I, and are one of the few doughboys or gobs who were actually in service for nineteen months — then, Grampa, you're in. You don't even have to raise radishes. The land is yours after sitting on it for seven months and constructing a habitable house.

If you were in service for less than nineteen months, but more than one year, you'll have to cultivate ¹⁄₁₆ of your acreage in the first three years before you get title to your land.

Unsurveyed Homesteads: If the land you pick out for your future home is unsurveyed — and 98 per cent of Alaska is unsurveyed — your residence and land improvement requirements will be the same, but the procedure will be slightly different.

Generally speaking, the unsurveyed land is farther out in the hinterland; not so close to "civilization" as the land which has already been classified and surveyed.

As soon as you've picked out your land, you may move onto it — that is, of course, if no one else is there first. Within ninety days you fill out a "Notice of Location" at the land office, and give the clerk a $10 filing fee and a description of your land. The description will probably read something like this:

"From the mouth of Trout Creek and Mosquito River 2640 feet due north, thence 2640 feet due west, thence 2640 feet due south, and 2640 feet due east to the point of beginning."

From there on in, your residence, land cultivation and other requirements are the same as for surveyed land.

When you submit your statement of Final Proof you will receive a free survey which Uncle must give you before you get your patent. Because of the limited budget for financing land surveys you may have to wait a year or more before the money is available to send a crew into your area to measure up your land.

After the survey is made, the surveyors draw up a plat of your land which is described in official aliquot terms, and you make "Application for Homestead." This costs $16.

From there on, the procedure is the same as for surveyed land.

You now know how to acquire 160 acres from Uncle Sam. But the physical and mental task of life in the bush is tough for many. Petty annoyances in the heart of civilization can become major frustrations in the heart of the wilderness. Like trying to start your car at 30 below where there's no garage to call or no way to call one. And there are emergencies when you have to find a bush pilot to fly you to the hospital in case of illness or accident.

But many a self-sufficient family has found that homesteading in the 49th state can be a rich and rewarding way of life. When you fly over the vast wilderness and see the many little clearings with a cabin or two, and smoke rising from the chimneys, it's obvious that the homesteader is playing a greater and greater part in the development of the far-flung north country. Every year more people are discovering that their 160 acres can be their land of opportunity.

9

The Straight Dope on Agriculture

"Are you going to give your readers the straight dope on farming in Alaska, or are you going to do what so many writers do — paint the bucket at the end of the rainbow?" asked Dr. Allan Mick, director of the University of Alaska's Agricultural Experiment Stations.

We sat in Dr. Mick's modern office in the recently constructed administration building at Palmer, in the heart of the Matanuska Valley. Mick is a personable young man who looks more like a college professor than a professional farmer. He came to Alaska in 1948, armed with a bachelor's degree in agricultural engineering and a Ph.D. in science, to serve as soil surveyor for the United States Department of Agriculture.

When Don Irwin retired in 1957, young Mick was named head of the Alaska Experiment Stations, and since that time has been a vital force in encouraging Alaska's farm production. According to agronomists across the country, the experiment stations and staff are doing an outstanding job of guiding the Alaskan farm economy to higher efficiency and greater stability.

"Farming in Alaska isn't really sixty-pound cabbages and strawberries as big as half a dollar," Mick stated frankly.

"If it were, we'd have a million farmers up here right now. It's true that we have some colossal vegetables at our state fairs, but they don't just happen. They're grown by experts especially for the show. The basic truth about Alaskan agriculture is just this:

"If you have enough money and experience to get into farming in Iowa today, then you may have enough money and experience to get into farming in Alaska."

He leaned back in his chair. "Or let me say it this way. If you can't make a success of farming in your own home county, then you had better not try farming in Alaska."

"Isn't that pretty strong medicine, Allan?" we asked him. "If that is the case, how do you account for Alaskan agricultural products having an annual retail value of better than ten million dollars — and the Matanuska Valley Co-op alone doing an annual gross business of seven million. You've even claimed that the over-all contribution of farming to Alaska's internal economy now exceeds twenty-five million a year."

Mick explained that there are about eight hundred farm families in Alaska at the present time who are selling commercially and doing a monumental job. Most of them are still small producers, but some have risen to the six-figures-a-year bracket. Those who are producing in a big way are on top because they've had adequate financing and superior know-how. They would succeed anywhere.

"You can't emphasize this too strongly," Mick stated. "Since statehood was voted by Congress we've received sacks and sacks of mail from bright-eyed eager souls planning to rush north and get rich quick off the farm. Most of them feel that in a year — or perhaps it'll take them two — they'll have fortunes sprouting from the soil."

These enthusiastic but ill-prepared argonauts are a special worry of Dr. Mick. "After all, farming in Alaska is a way of life, not a way to get rich quick," he said strongly. "If you're geared to farming, dairying or animal husbandry, and you're young enough and properly financed, then Alaska may have what you're looking for.

"But if you're a newspaperman or a factory worker, and decide it's time for a change to the soil, don't rush north to Matanuska."

Far too many families in the other states quit their jobs, pull up stakes, pile their kids into the old jalopy, paint a sign on it saying "ALASKA OR BUST," and head north.

After a year or so the husband charges into Mick's office and blows his stack. "Why in hell don't the gov'ment or somebody tell us the real stuff about Alaska? That land out there's no damn good!"

It's a waste of breath to tell him where the trouble lies, Mick implies. "I just say I hear they're hiring help at that new missile anti-missile base. If he can get a job with lots of overtime he'll be able to send the wife and kids back home in a few months and get back himself before next winter."

Alaska is a johnny-come-lately in the agricultural picture. The lower 48 states were settled by land-hungry migrants who tilled their living from the soil. The soil was the beginning of things American. It was the growth factor of the new nation.

In Alaska the American procedure was reversed. It was furs and salmon and gold that brought men north and kept them on the move. The philosophy of the early adventurers up here "to get-it-and-get-out" was not conducive to any long-range endeavor like agriculture. Those who had farms often quit the fields to go fishing in Bristol Bay or mining in the hills.

With the population shifting with each new gold strike and the vagaries of the salmon, it was more profitable to bring in produce from the Outside to each current metropolis than to till the soil and grow food in Alaska.

Father Hilscher made a sizable gold strike in the Klondike, but early in the game he discovered there was more money in feeding the goldseekers than in putting down potholes for himself. He brought in beefsteaks on the hoof down the Yukon and over the Valdez trail and sold meat to the miners in the Fortymile, and to the gold camp of Fairbanks.

That was in the good old days of 1898-1912. Today Alaska is still importing 95 per cent of her meat, 70 per cent of her milk, and 85 per cent of her fresh produce.

The present rapid increase in Alaska's resident population — and the ever-increasing migration north — is widening even more the gap between what Alaska produces and what Alaska eats. Herein lies the opportunity for the experienced farmer.

"Only about twenty-two thousand of the million accessible acres suitable for agriculture have been cleared for cultivation," Dr. Mick said. "The reason why is simple. Land clearing comes high up here — from seventy-five to a hundred and fifty dollars per acre is needed to scrape off and burn the trees and prepare the first seed bed."

Up in the Tanana Valley a blue-eyed, long-term farmer by the name of Paul Elbert is working out an idea which he thinks will drop land-clearing prices into the bargain basement. Taking a tip from the DEW Line contractors, who have been stripping the tundra for their radar sites, he purchased "the biggest earthworm tractor Alexander P. Botts ever dreamed of," and started on a revolutionary method of forest annihilation.

Most tractors are driven ahead and backed up, and driven ahead and backed up again until the field is cleared. But Elbert's tractor starts a circle at the outside perimeter of a 20- or 30-acre piece of land and goes round and round without stopping until it gets to the center of the field. The 8-foot-high blade is adjusted like a snowplow and it rolls large trees, brush, willows and moss into a great circular windrow.

When the windrow is dry, he lights a fire at one end, like a Chinese punk, and the flame spirals round and round until the entire field is cleared of debris.

"It saves time, it saves money, and it may be the answer to our land-clearing problems," Mick remarked. "But so far Elbert's experiment has a couple of drawbacks. One is the original cost of the tractor which is in the neighborhood of fifty-five thousand dollars, and will take a considerable number of land-clearing jobs to pay for. The other is that the tractor is expensive to operate and maintain in good repair.

"But if it works out, it could even result in more acreage being made available for farming than the present economy can absorb," Mick admitted.

There is one drawback to farming in Alaska which must be taken into consideration before anyone casts his lot with the soil in the new state. Farm labor costs are very high. This unnatural situation has been brought on by the crash military programs building up the defenses of the northern frontier. These military installations had to be built regardless of cost, and labor was recruited and siphoned from industry everywhere — including the farms of Alaska.

Why should Joe Blow, for example, work twelve to fifteen hours a day on a dairy farm in the Matanuska Valley for $75 a week when he can get two or three times that amount at a defense installation? Until economic conditions adjust themselves, farming in Alaska will be most successful as a family industry.

About 99 per cent of the letters coming into Dr. Mick's office want information on the "best place to farm."

"That's like asking me whether it's better to live in New York or Florida," Mick smiled. "Alaska's scattered farming areas have different climates, different soil conditions and different agricultural potentials. For the farm family of today, looking for a site to establish a 'dynasty' for the next generation or two, it's better to look at *all* of Alaska's farm possibilities before unloading the plow and the family."

Each section of Alaska has its advantages and disadvantages. The Matanuska area and the farms around the big market of Anchorage have the largest farm population and grow 67 per cent of all the agricultural products sold in Alaska. The Tanana Valley around Fairbanks is next with 16 per cent. The Kenai, Kodiak Island and the Aleutian wool ventures account for 8 per cent of the annual cash crop. Other areas throughout the state make up the remaining 9 per cent.

Alaska's climates and its growing seasons are described in the chart on page 116. "Please note particularly the long hours of sunshine in the summer, as we will discuss this high-latitude phenomenon later on," Mick pointed out.

"You'll see that Southeastern Alaska has a mild climate, almost like the Pacific Northwest," Mick indicated with his pencil. "It has considerable rain, moderate snow, and the trees grow thick and straight — with land-clearing costs extra high.

WEATHER DATA

Place	Extremes* High	Low	For the frost-free season only Start[1]	Length[1]	Max.[2]	Min.[2]	Rain	Sunshine[3]
	F°	F°	Date	Days	F°	F°	Inches	Hours
Matanuska-Susitna Area								
Anchorage	86	−38	5/21	113	64	46	6	8–17
Palmer	87	−42	5/30	100	66	42	10	10–17
Matanuska	91	−41	5/28	105	66	45	7	9–17
Tanana Valley								
Fairbanks	93	−66	5/21	101	68	49	6	9–21
Big Delta	90	−63	5/21	100	66	44	7	10–20
Nenana	98	−66	5/20	98	70	46	5	12–19
Kenai Peninsula								
Homer	79	−18	5/31	107	58	41	7	8–17
Kenai	87	−48	6/17	72	61	45	6	7–17
Seward	84	−29	5/17	135	59	45	6	6–16
Southeastern Alaska								
Juneau	87	−10	4/22	183	59	44	29	5–15
Petersburg	84	−19	5/18	138	61	45	33	4–16
Kodiak-Aleutian Islands								
Kodiak	81	−5	5/1	167	53	45	29	5–15
Unalaska Island	80	5	5/18	133	56	44	14	5–14

* These two columns give the coldest winter temperature on record and the highest summer temperature.
[1] Average date of the last frost in spring, and length of frost-free period in days, respectively.
[2] Average maximum and minimum temperature during the frost-free season.
[3] The first value is the average actual hours of daily sunshine while the second figure gives the possible hours of daily sunshine.

The Cathedral of Saint Michael at Sitka Holds Many
Early-day Russian Treasures

Wyman, Fairbanks

Fairbanks Is the Heart of Central Alaska

Anchorage, Largest City in the New State

Mac's Foto, Anchorage

Capital City of Juneau (*above*) Lies at the Water's Edge, beneath the Steep Slopes of Mt. Juneau. Mt. McKinley (*below*), Highest Peak in North America, from Wonder Lake.

Mac's Foto, Anch...

Tourist Ship in Glacier Bay

Winter Carnival Sled Dog Races, Fairbanks

Machetanz, Pa...

Mac's Foto, Anchorage

The Alaska Railroad along Turnagain Arm

Alaska Has But 5000 Miles of Road

Mac's Foto, Anchorage

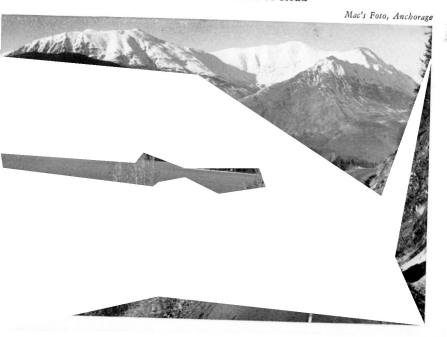

Northern Consolidated Airlin

"No Fishing Like Alaskan Fishing," Sportsmen Declare

Bathing Beach, Goose Lake, City of Anchorage

Mac's Foto, Anchor

Mac's Foto, Anchorage

Dungeness Crabs Are an Important Industry
at Petersburg and Cordova

A Salmon Seiner at Work

Fish and Wildlife Service

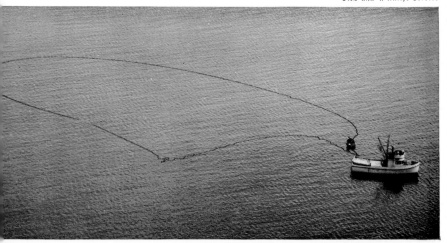

With the Greatest of Ease. This Eskimo Miss Is Tossed High into the Air During the Blanket Toss Exhibition at the Anchorage Fur Rendezvous.

This and other Eskimo sports are highlighted during the annual week-long winter festival held in February, which in 1959 was Alaska's "first" Statehood celebration party. Each year this "Mardi Gras of the North" attracts many visitors from the south 48 states, as well as from all over Alaska.

Pacific Northern Airlines

Trawling for King Crab Is a New Industry in Alaska

Wakefield's Deep Sea Trawlers, I

Marion Johnson Qualified to Join the Kodiak Skin Divers' Club
by Bringing Up a Four-Foot King Crab

Digging Potatoes in the Matanuska Valley

World's Largest Platinum Dredge, at Platinum, Alaska

Alaska's First Pulp Plant, at Ketchikan

Gold Mining Is Still a Romantic Business

Mac's Foto, Anchorage

Portage Glacier is a Tourist Attraction near Anchorage

Proposed Rampart Power Site on the Yukon River

U.S. Army

Mac's Foto, Anchorage

Eskimos Are the Travelin'est People —
They Have Great Pride in Their Native Culture and Apparel

Anchorage International Airport Is Host to Eighteen Airlines

Mac's Foto, Anchorage

Standard Oil Co. of Califor
Western Operations, Inc., Ward W

Swanson River Unit #2,
Second Producing Well on the Kenai Peninsula

Mac's Foto, Anchorage

Freight Transportation on Alaska's Rivers Is Now by Diesel Pushers

Love on the Pribilof Islands

Fish and Wildlife Service

DEW Line Radomes and White Alice Antennas
Stand Guard in the Arctic

"There are lots of islands in the Panhandle, and much of the land is vertical, so your best bet down here is truck gardening.

"Central Alaska, on the other hand, has a continental climate — hot in summer, cold in winter," he explained. "Being north of the Alaska Range, this area doesn't have the moderating influences of the Japanese Current and the Pacific Ocean.

"The growing season is short here, but the warmer temperatures and the long hours of summer sunshine cause crops to mature faster than along the coast," Mick said. "Many people think that this Tanana-Yukon Valley, which has a marketing center in Fairbanks and nearby airbases, will eventually be a vast farming-livestock region.

"Southcentral Alaska, which has several distinct farming areas, has a slightly longer growing season than Central Alaska, but fewer hours of sunshine," Mick continued.

"Kodiak Island has proved itself as a cattle-growing area; however, the market here is small, and products must be transported to the more populous Anchorage area.

"The same marketing conditions exist on the productive Kenai Peninsula. There is good soil here, and miles of lush grass for cattle grazing, but the market is far away. Beef and potatoes must be trucked to Anchorage — a long haul compared to bringing produce to Anchorage from the Matanuska Valley. But with oil on the Kenai, who knows — the market may suddenly spout like a gusher.

"The Matanuska Valley farmers have readymade markets, being close to Anchorage, Fort Richardson and Elmendorf Air Force Base," Mick continued. "Agriculture is well established here. Most good farm land is in private hands, and the best acreage now in use sells for an average of two hundred dollars per acre. Many newcomers find it's cheaper to buy tillable land than to go through the long, hard process of homesteading, land-clearing and getting the soil ready for cultivation."

Alaska's major farm product is milk, but at present only about 30 per cent of the milk consumed in the Northland comes from local dairies. To meet the demand, vast quantities of evaporated, powdered and concentrated milk are shipped in from the Outside.

Many children born and raised in Alaska get accustomed to canned milk and refuse to drink anything else. This is usually a source of much embarrassment when traveling Outside where only fresh milk is available in restaurants.

Our daughter Hilary, when she was three years old, demanded canned milk at a hotel in Minneapolis. It caused a lot of talk among the dining room staff, and finally the chef came out of the kitchen to see the Alaskan child who drank only *canned* milk — heresy in the heart of the dairy country.

To help Alaskans corner a bigger share of the milk market, Dr. Mick and his staff are busily strengthening and upgrading the dairy industry in the new state.

"As a result of scientific breeding and efficient management, the average Alaskan cow now produces over ninety-five hundred pounds of milk per year, compared to a U.S. average of five thousand pounds," Mick explained proudly. "A good many of our cows go to fifteen thousand pounds and better."

At this writing, dairymen in the Matanuska Valley get $9 per hundred weight for 4 per cent milk. Efficient operators produce this milk for $6. The net profit buys many things that make life in Alaska more enjoyable.

"Farmers up here now realize that there is no profit in investing five hundred dollars in a cull cow," said Dr. Mick. "After all, the cost of shipping a nondescript, low-producing cow up from the Midwest is just as high as shipping up a good one, and it isn't very profitable as far as milk is concerned.

"Much of Alaska's dairy stock improvement has come about as the result of the Matanuska Experiment Station's stud herd of eleven high-priced, registered bulls — Holsteins, Guernseys and Red Danes.

"We've worked out a system with the farmers in this area so that about eighty per cent of the dairy herds can be serviced by artificial insemination," Mick stated.

"The station has men on call around the clock, three hundred sixty-five days of the year, just to take care of the valley's cows," the director explained. "Every dairyman has been taught to watch his herd meticulously. If a cow needs servicing, the farmer calls the station at any hour of the day or night, and a technician experienced in artificial insemination is on the way with a small vial of semen mixed with egg white. One batch of semen, properly treated with egg white, will stay potent for about five days, and will take care of eight to ten cows."

Farmers living farther away from Palmer may get a stud bull "on loan." And several times a year prize bulls are transported over the highway from Palmer to the Experiment Station at College, near Fairbanks, to service the dairy industry of the Tanana Valley. Rural residents are getting used to seeing a 2000-pound Holstein gentleman enjoying the beautiful mountainous scenery as he speeds along from one rural chore to another.

But a laboratory test-tube may soon make these trips unnecessary and even obsolete, Dr. Mick predicted. What's more, it could even make Alaska a bull-less state!

Experiments have shown that semen frozen to 170 degrees below zero will keep its potency indefinitely. Thus world-premier bulls in Wisconsin could provide the life-giving spark to herds throughout the nation and eventually any place in the world. Arrangements are now being made to transport shipments of 170-below sperm to Alaska to try out on herds up here.

An even more startling development in improving dairy stock is now being tried in the States and may some day be used in Alaska, Mick said. Semen from prized sires will be inseminated into cows whose milk production is more than 15,000 pounds per year. Pregnancy tests will be made to establish the existence of an embryo. When the embryo is 27 days old it will be transplanted surgically into a mediocre or cull cow for the completion of the gestation period.

All heredity characteristics will be in the embryo, and the cull cow will be merely the vehicle for the completion of the pregnancy cycle. The result will be a prize, registered calf, and the high-milk-producing dam may be utilized several times a year for this artificial upgrading of Alaskan dairy herds.

Though milk production has made great strides in the new state, poultry and egg producers have found the going rough. Some of the farmers are raising larger flocks for increased efficiency, but feed is expensive and local eggs must compete with airborne and express eggs shipped from the other states and Canada. These imported eggs, while generally of poorer quality, undersell the local products as loss leaders in the supermarkets. The same is true of broilers and fryers. Few local chickens are on the market. But as the volume of grain grown in Alaska increases, the prospects for poultry and egg production should improve.

Dr. Mick has twenty-one men on his staff in Palmer and five at the Experiment Station at College working on animal husbandry and agriculture.

"Right now forty per cent of Alaska's farm income is from potatoes," Dr. Mick said. "We're spending a lot of time improving the varieties we have and developing new ones which could make Alaska the potato state of the nation.

"About half of the potatoes grown in the Northland are still the famous Arctic Seedlings, improved by Don Irwin, Director Emeritus of Alaska Experiment Stations," Mick pointed out. "But Alaska's farmers now have three or four other varieties which are doing well. Teton seems to be a ringrot-resistant variety that is a consistent producer. Up in Fairbanks, John Holm likes Canus, a fine, mealy variety, low in sugar content, which is excellent for potato chips and French fries. Other farmers grow our new numbered varieties which we call only #114 and #43.

"To develop #114, our potato breeders screened out more than twenty-seven thousand seedlings from cross-pollinated plants. These were selected down to about one thousand; then the final selection had to be increased to get enough seed for our commercial growers in the valley. But it'll take six to eight years to show whether they're as good as we think they are.

"We've learned it never pays to announce results until we've completely finished a study," Dr. Mick chuckled. "A number of years ago several carloads of our new Knik potato were sold to the Army. This potato — named after the town of Knik, the Knik River, the Knik Glacier and the Knik Indians — had been grown for a number of years, was smooth and firm, and kept exceptionally well.

"But one day we got a call from the quartermaster that burned the telephone to a crisp," Mick recalled with a grimace.

"What in hell are your farmers trying to do — selling us black potatoes?"

Investigation revealed that the Kniks had been dumped into huge bins — without proper ventilation. This, plus the weight of the potatoes, caused them to generate within themselves minute quantities of monoxide gas (utterly innocuous to humans) which turned the potatoes black.

"But there was a happy sequel to that black potato incident," Mick smiled broadly. "The U.S. Department of Agriculture never likes to get into a Donnybrook with the Army — especially over the purchase of foodstuffs in Alaska — so the black potatoes resulted in a substantial appropriation for continuous research on potato culture in the northern latitudes.

"In achieving a long-range agricultural economy in Alaska, the 49th state must develop something on an exclusive — or preferential — basis," Mick said. "Like California oranges, Oregon pears, Washington apples, Georgia peaches, Iowa corn or Missouri mules.

"Earlier I remarked about the long days of sunlight in the high latitudes and their importance in agriculture up here. Alaska's preferential products can well stem from special enterprises that can make use of excessive sunlight as its ace-in-the-hole. Up here we have several native grasses that ripen seed *only* in a short, fast-growing season with fifteen to twenty hours of sunlight," Mick elaborated. "In the lower latitudes of the other states these fast-growing grasses will flourish but not seed. From a cattleman's point of view, a tall grass that will maintain its vigor and not go to seed is ideal cattle food.

"From an Alaskan point of view it's ideal, too," he said. "A grass seed industry might provide a continuing economy, because new seed will be needed each spring for Stateside planting."

There are a number of plants native to Alaska which will grow also in the lower latitudes but won't blossom and reseed. One of these is a dwarf bentgrass which looks ideally suited to producing velvety-smooth golf courses.

"Someday we hope to advertise that Alaskan bentgrass makes your lawnmower obsolete," Mick laughed. "I wish that something like that had happened in my youth. The varieties our agronomists are now studying grow perhaps an inch high. When perfected, this bentgrass seed industry may be as important to Alaskans as the tulip bulb industry is to Holland or the daffodil fields to Puget Sound."

Another exciting discovery has been in Alaska pharmacopoeia. Several varieties of sagebrush with definite medical importance have been found, and a long-range research program is under way. Nicotine-bearing plants grown in northern latitudes have been found to produce far greater yields of nicotine than those in lower latitudes, and this might be of decisive economic value to insecticide manufacturers.

Although most areas of the Big Part of Alaska have been dubbed too rigorous for orchard crops — apples, pears, cherries — some of the hardier varieties of crabapples mature. The Experiment Stations and many farmers are experimenting with other fruit trees especially adapted to withstand our northern winters.

"With this hardy stock, Alaska may have a future in

supplying virus-free scion stock for fruit trees," Mick said. "Horticulturists throughout the country who want fine orchards don't grow fruit trees from seed — they build their trees in stages. Each tree is really three trees in one: the rootstock, the trunk or scion stock, and the bearing part or headstock.

"The technique is to take the superior rootstock of one variety, graft onto it the tough, disease-resistant scion stock of another specie, and onto that graft the bearing part of a tree which will determine the variety of apple, pear or other fruit the tree is to produce.

"Perhaps in the future Alaska scion stock will be in demand in Outside nurseries because it is resistant to a score of perils which plague many orchard crops.

"Nursery stock for sale outside Alaska can be another money-maker for the farmer," Dr. Mick went on. "Like so many of our plants up here, our nursery stock is climatically very hardy and particularly disease-resistant.

"These are just a few of the future agricultural possibilities in the state of Alaska," Allan Mick summarized. "There are dozens of others waiting to be uncovered. Newcomers to the state would do well to investigate these possibilities thoroughly and consider a long-range farm program based on products that will be exclusively Alaskan."

Have we painted the pot at the end of the rainbow in iridescent colors? We don't think so.

The opportunities for making a success in farming in the new state are limitless — bounded only by your own vision, ability, financing and desire to work. But, as we have pointed out, farming in Alaska is not for the uninitiated.

Farming has become big business in the Matanuska Valley since the frustrating days of the original ill-prepared Matanuska Colony a quarter of a century ago. And it's become a specialized endeavor in the Tanana Valley where once the old Sourdoughs tried out a few spuds and radishes.

"We expect to make farming a much greater part of Alaska's economy in years to come," Dr. Mick stressed. "The scientists working up here are finding great rewards in helping the northern farmer to expand his knowledge and push back the last agricultural frontier."

10

Four-legged Farming

I GUESS IT WAS ABOUT TWENTY YEARS AGO WHEN
I first said that some day the United States would recognize
Alaska as one of the finest places in the world to grow wool
and raise mutton," I. M. C. Anderson remarked in his slow,
Western drawl.

"Right now, out there on the Aleutian Chain, where the
temperature stays just about the same the year around, sheep
raising is proving to be mighty encouraging."

This remark is an understatement coming from Alaska's
Number One animal husbandryman whose prophecies for
the success of livestock, dairying, wool growing and lamb
production have hit the bull's-eye continuously for the past
twenty-some years.

If it weren't for Andy's faith in the Aleutians and his constant encouragement of sheep farming out toward the western extremity of the state of Alaska, this area would have
little economic value. Its importance would be limited to
DEW Line radar installations, ICBM sites, landing fields en
route to the Orient, several naval bases and breeding grounds
of the almost extinct sea otter. Even the Aleuts had just
about abandoned their poor villages on the Chain in ex-

change for employment around Uncle Sam's defense locations.

With the increase in sheep on the islands, some of the Aleuts have taken training in sheepmanship and make excellent ranchers. "Some of them can shear a hundred sheep in one day, and that's better than par for the course on any range," Andy remarked.

Even before our GI troops took over the bleak, windy Aleutians in 1942, Isaac Milton Compton Anderson advocated putting sheep to pasture on this long expanse of broken-up land that stretches into the Pacific Ocean a time zone farther west than Hawaii.

Anderson is so respected and revered by farmers and livestock men throughout Alaska that one homesteader in the Tanana Valley who had never heard of Adak — let alone Attu — declared, "If Andy says to put sheep on the Aleutians, then that's a good place to put sheep!"

His confidence in Andy was well grounded. Today sheep are thriving on "those wonderful, treeless islands where the temperature, though cool, is constant almost all year round, and the range is principally tall, waving grass." The sheep produce wool of such superior quality that it commands a premium price when delivered to market in the other states. This more than pays for the long transportation haul. Each year over 100,000 pounds of Aleutian wool are shipped to the Portland, Oregon, market, and most of it is processed by the Oregon Worsted Mills.

"Out in the Aleutians, wool grows twelve months around the calendar," Andy announced dryly, then went on to explain. "Here's what happens. Take Western range wool from Montana and Oregon. It develops a weak spot in the fiber because of the sharp difference in temperature between the hard winters and hot summers. Seems as if it stops growing when the seasons change.

"The fine, uniform fiber of the Alaskan wool is due to the even, year-around climate. That's why we say that Aleutian wool grows the year around.

"There's another reason for the high value of Aleutian wool," Andy went on. "It has the least shrinkage of any wool known on the American market. Now a hundred pounds of Western range wool will shrink down to only thirty or forty pounds of clean wool after it has been washed and all the dirt, grease and sand are scrubbed out. Aleutian sheep are so clean that one hundred pounds of fleece wool produce from sixty to seventy pounds of scoured wool. So you see there's only about thirty to forty pounds of Alaskan real estate in our wool.

"Actually, most of the wool, when it comes right off the sheep, looks so clean you would swear it had already been washed."

Some of the meat from these Aleutian sheep is now being flown to Anchorage by Reeve Aleutian Airways, and the demand has been so encouraging that local residents put in their orders in advance. "You've never lived until you've tasted the succulent Aleutian lamb chops," Andy declared. "They're strictly for the Alaskan gourmet! There's something about the Aleutian range, which consists of grass and herbs, that gives the meat a better flavor than that of sheep raised on grass and shrubs of the Western range.

"Aleutian mutton tastes much like the coveted bighorn and Dall sheep meat, and if you have ever eaten roasts from these superb game animals you know what I'm talking about," Andy said. "Even the old ewes and wethers have a fine flavor — none of the acrid mutton taste you occasionally get from the grandparents of the Western range."

Aleutian sheep grow bigger than the same varieties in the other states, the wethers and rams averaging from ten to forty pounds more per animal. Where ewes elsewhere weigh from 90 to 115 pounds, in Alaska they tip the scales at 120 to 140 pounds. Those extra pounds of meat are extra profit for the Alaskan sheep farmer. In many cases they account for part of the black ink on the operation.

The increase in flocks out on the Chain is high — from 65 to 80 per cent per year, Andy explained. Ewes are bred in December and January to lamb in May and June. On the Aleutians there is no big game — no bears or wolves — and the sole predators are the fox and the raven, which are bothersome only during the lambing season. The foxes will steal the newborn kits, and the ravens pick out the eyes of the babes, leaving them to die. But good marksmanship on the part of the sheepherders has kept the mortality rate to a minimum.

There seems to be another reason for the increase in Aleutian flocks, according to Anderson. No one knows whether it's the climate or what, but during the short breeding season a hundred rams will expertly take care of two thousand ewes. During the sixty-day mating season those rams never miss a single ewe — if she's interested.

Many varieties of sheep have been tried on the Chain. But the most satisfactory has been the Columbia breed, started on the King Ranch in Wyoming and perfected at the U.S. Sheep Breeding Station at Dubois, Idaho.

At present there are substantial sheep ranches on Umnak and Unalaska, smaller flocks on Chirikof, Uganik and Harvester islands. But there's room for thousands more sheep on those practically uninhabited lands pointing out to Siberia. All of the islands west of Kodiak are treeless, and most of them are blessed with a thick covering of nutritious grass which keeps the sheep self-supporting the year around.

This natural forage which has proven such a boon to the sheep industry can also make Alaska one of the great cattle-producing areas of the world, Andy predicts. And Andy never makes a prognostication until he has studied the situation from all angles. Because of the success of his predictions over many years, his reputation as Alaska's foremost authority on animal husbandry has spread to the other states. He has the advantage over other animal husbandrymen who come north — he not only knows his livestock but he knows Alaska, all of Alaska.

Andy has been a livestock man all his life. He was born on a cattle ranch in eastern Oregon, was graduated from Oregon State College in animal husbandry, and spent years helping settlers in Oregon, Idaho and Montana with their cattle problems.

"During the drought and depression of the '30s, things were tough on the dry land of Montana," Andy reminisced. "Any help we county agents could give a settler in saving his animals was the difference between a farmer's keeping his land and family together — or another mortgage foreclosed. Our hearts were in our work to help those people make a go of it on the frontier."

When the chance came to take charge of animal husbandry at the University of Alaska Experiment Station at College, it was a challenge Andy couldn't pass up.

"The missus and I bundled our possessions and our kiddies together and headed north," he said. "That was over twenty years ago and we never regretted the move. Here was a new land, new people and new horizons to sharpen our teeth on."

Andy studied the climate, the grasses, the range, the forage — every phase of the animal husbandry game. Slowly he came to the conclusion that great parts of the Northland could be profitably utilized for basic food production.

He also came to the conclusion that the main reasons for failure in the early attempts at sheep and cattle raising in Alaska were inexperience and lack of capital.

"Being a successful four-legged farmer is just like being a successful auto mechanic," he philosophized. "You've got to know what you're doing, or it is going to cost you nothing but money and heartache. All too often the farmer or rancher who goes broke up here blames the country and the climate and the town banker — anything and everybody but himself and his inexperience."

After five years with the University of Alaska Experiment Station, helping uninitiated and inexperienced farmers with their problems, Andy became Alaska Representative for the Farm Security Administration, later known as the Farmers Home Administration. For fourteen years he traveled over all Alaska, and got to know every farmer and homesteader.

When he retired from government service in 1956, Andy was asked to be livestock buyer and advisor for groups of farmers in Alaska. The demand for his services grew, and today he is Alaska's Number One dealer in beef, dairy cows and sheep. He is also consultant to several Stateside companies now active in the sheep and cattle business in Alaska.

Through Andy's encouragement, the livestock industry is on the increase in several parts of the north country. It has a chance of becoming one of Alaska's most stable industries.

Alaska today imports almost $20,000,000 in meat and meat products each year from the other states and Canada. Andy says, with the same degree of authority with which he discusses sheep in the Aleutians, "The 49th state can, and will, supply a good share of the meat we will need to feed our growing population.

"We have millions of acres for open range, we have grasses and grains, and we have the right kind of climate.

"Just to show you what I mean, you ride the streamliner of the Alaska Railroad from Anchorage to Fairbanks. That's three hundred and seventy-one miles. Except for the short distance through the mountains, have you ever seen better summer rangeland anywhere?

"In the bottomland, you can harvest a fine stand of native hay by the Fourth of July, and the native grasses are high in protein until the frost knocks them down in the fall," Andy stated.

"But equally as important as the rangeland is the vast acreage available for grain farming," he explained. "This grain is necessary to 'finish off' livestock before it goes to market.

"Barley does exceptionally well up here, and annual production runs from thirty-five to eighty bushels per acre! Nowhere is there a higher nutritive content than in grains grown in these northern latitudes, and miles and miles of level valley land can grow barley for cattle feed.

"I don't think we will have to wait too long to see farms of a thousand acres of barley in the Tanana Valley around Fairbanks," he stated. "The new state has a hundred and three million acres of land as a dowry from Uncle Sam. It can sell the land in large chunks. That is what is needed to do an efficient job of barley farming and cattle feeding."

Perhaps, like Andy, you have to be a bit visionary to see

all this coming. But you can take it right out of the pages of the settling of the West.

"Now let's go a step farther," Andy said as he sat back and smiled slowly. "As soon as the railroad from the States to Alaska is built, the 49th state will enter another phase of four-legged farming. Cattle ranchers in the other states who are now short on summer range will send steers by the train-load to the Central and Southcentral districts of Alaska.

"The natural brome grasses will put weight on the steers at the rate of two and a half pounds per day," Andy predicted. "Then in the fall they will be marbled on Alaska barley and be ready for the market when they are needed.

"I've had lots of people agree that Central Alaska would make a wonderful place to graze cattle in summer," Andy continued, "but they turn skeptical about any winter ranging. Who could afford barns and feed for a thousand or so head of cattle?

"So I tell them what I learned years ago in Montana. Where buffalo can get along by themselves Hereford cattle can get along with a little help. By this, I mean winter shelters where they can get out of the wind and feed and bed down on dry ground."

Then Andy explained about the buffalo that were turned loose back in 1928 in the Big Delta country, ninety miles south of Fairbanks, where the mercury drops to 50 below in the winter. The bison got so numerous they became a menace on the Alaska Highway, and one grizzled old gentle-man disputed the center of the blacktop with several tourist automobiles, much to the detriment of the products of Detroit.

Airplane pilots coming in for a landing would have to radio

the tower at Big Delta to "Shoo those damned buffalo off the runway." Finally the Fish and Wildlife had to establish a "selective hunting" of surplus males to cut down the herd.

"I guess you could say those buffalo got along by themselves all right," Andy chuckled. "And I feel that large herds of cattle would have no trouble wintering over here with a little assistance."

Wherever there is homesteading in Alaska — and that includes the Kenai Peninsula, the Matanuska Valley, the Susitna Flats, the Copper River country and the broad reaches of the Tanana and Yukon valleys — there you will find starter herds of livestock. The Alaska climate seems to be perfect for cattle propagation. For some reason that might have to do with the midnight sun or the northern lights, annual calf production is 90 per cent or better up here. Beef herds double in size the good old natural way.

The Scotch Highland and the Hereford bulls seem particularly efficient. But for some reason, the Black Angus bulls, when they fill up on daisies and wildflowers (and there are lots of wildflowers in Alaska), act like Ferdinand and forget to rustle the business for which nature intended them.

In the Matanuska Valley and in Anchorage there are certificated abattoirs which do custom slaughtering of beef, and you can pick out your winter's supply of beef while it's still on the hoof. Anchorage has a butcher shop that specializes in meats which are grown in Alaska.

The island of Kodiak is unique in the cattle picture. Here two separate branches of the federal government have carried on a running feud over whether the beef cattle or the Kodiak brown bear should rule the range.

Ever since the establishment of a U.S. Department of Agriculture Experiment Station on Kodiak near the turn of the century, beef animals have done well there. Lush meadows fattened cattle in summer and an abundance of beach rye sustained them through the winter. During the war days, when steaks were hard to get even in Kansas City, Kodiak never ran out.

As the beeves increased, they were menaced by the Kodiak brown bear, the largest carnivorous animal on earth. When the cattlemen went out after the brownies with shooting irons, they were stopped by the Fish and Wildlife Service, which was protecting its 1500-pound pets for posterity and the big game hunter.

By federal regulation, the brown bears of Kodiak are a privileged, pampered lot. A cattle rancher is not legally allowed to kill them even to protect his herd. All he is legally permitted to do when he finds a cow or two gutted by an antisocial brownie is to complain bitterly to Fish and Wildlife.

But Fish and Wildlife agents cannot be omnipresent, and after two or three cases of mysterious lead poisoning during the season the bruin tribe usually learns that it's healthier on the other side of the island.

In spite of bears and government agencies there are now five companies in the livestock business on Kodiak, with about two thousand head of cattle. Only recently more than fifty head of white-faced Herefords were sent to the Anchorage market, and no finer beeves came off the Texas range. They were fat and in excellent condition.

There is a horse farm on Kodiak, and range riding has become a popular recreation for the residents.

No account of beef and bulls in Alaska would be complete without the story of Chirikof Island. This large, grass-covered island stands about eighty miles out to sea southwest of Kodiak. In the mid-'80s it was visited occasionally by whalers who stopped to refill their fresh-water casks en route to the Bering Sea.

This was in the days before refrigeration, and ship crews subsisted mainly on salt pork and beef in brine. Mariners were constantly in danger of scurvy, and in those days the best-known antidote for this dread dietetic disease was fresh meat and raw potatoes.

As Chirikof was uninhabited, and had no predators, one of the San Francisco whaling companies decided this would be a good place to plant a few cows and a bull and let nature take its happy course. What could be more profitable than to have a private source of fresh beef halfway from San Francisco to the ice floes of the Bering Sea?

About the time six cows and a bull were put ashore at Chirikof, someone in Pittsburgh started manufacturing *steel* stays for milady's corsets. Whalebone became passé, and the whalers went no more to the Bering Sea.

But the beeves on Chirikof continued to prosper and propagate. An occasional sailing ship sniped a carcass off the island, but by and large the cattle were unmolested for more than forty years. They became wilder than gazelles, and constant inbreeding made serious inroads on the quality of the stock.

Several starts were made to capitalize on this "ownerless" beef, but lack of capital and the difficulty of transportation defeated every attempt. Chirikof had no harbor, and storms blew up quickly.

Then along came the fabulous Jack McCord who turned his unusual talents to the problem. Every old-time Alaskan knows Jack McCord as an incurable optimist and promoter par excellence. Jack saw a fortune in the cattle and acquired a long-time lease to Chirikof Island and its occupants from Uncle Sam.

But despite deals with several operators, Jack was stymied like the others by lack of capital, lack of refrigeration facilities and the difficulty of transportation. He finally gave up his lease on Chirikof and transferred his operations to Sitkalidak Island nearer Kodiak.

An operator from the state of Washington took over Chirikof, and today the herd, which had variously been estimated at five hundred to three thousand, depending on who was telling the story, has been culled out, cleaned up and improved. The improvement started with the elimination of home-grown bulls and the importation of registered Hereford sires. A fleet of made-over B-25 bombers now flies freshly killed beef from Chirikof to Anchorage, where it is chilled and aged and put on the retail market.

Throughout Alaska, wherever there are farms, you'll find rotund, prolific pigs. There are also a growing number of pork farms throughout the state which are furnishing juicy pork roasts, hams and spiced sausages to local markets.

Some of the best-fed pigs in the world live near Alaska's military bases, storing up calorie after calorie from the mess hall table scraps. The daily quantity of calories supplied each GI up here is 25 per cent higher than in military messes in less rigorous latitudes, and what the GI doesn't eat, Mr. Porker adds to his perimeter.

Any farmer in Alaska knows that a piglet who greets this world before the first of May will dress out well over two hundred pounds before Christmas. During the long summer days he can eat out of his well-filled trough practically twenty-four hours around the clock. This he does with noisy relish. Then, stretching his hide to the limit, he generally manages to put away a topping of grain and meal before he becomes genuine Alaskan pork chops or a fresh ham roast for Christmas.

An animal native to Alaska, but extinct in its wild state here for almost one hundred years, is the musk ox. And a much misunderstood and much maligned character is he.

Musk oxen lived on the Arctic slopes of Alaska, Canada, the Arctic islands and Greenland, but were exterminated in Alaska by the early whalers who prized the meat. In the mid-'20s thirty-four musk oxen were purchased from Greenland and brought to the University of Alaska to start a flourishing new wool industry in the Interior. The musk ox has a thick undercoat of lightest-weight, cashmere-type wool called qiviut. But the experiment was not a success. Inexperienced and uninterested help decided that the shaggy beasts were antisocial, that they were a menace, and that they were not the answer to Alaska's meat and wool problems.

So after utterly inconclusive attempts at educating the Arctic animals how to act on the campus, the lot of them were shipped off to Nunivak Island in the Bering Sea and committed — horns, wool and meat — to the gentle mercies of the Fish and Wildlife Service. Nature took over and today, despite some illegal hunting, the wild and woolly herd which no man can get near numbers over two hundred fifty.

Through encouragement of John J. Teal, Jr., director of the Institute of Northern Agricultural Research, the University of Alaska may soon give the musk ox another chance. Teal, who has studied the musk ox for years, transported some calves to his Vermont farm and was delighted to find them friendly and intelligent. If domesticated from birth, he reported, they're easy to handle and gentle as lambs. They follow Teal's children around and even take a dip with the family in the old swimming hole.

Teal may furnish the University of Alaska with musk oxen for experimentation, and he hopes they'll beget many more which can be parceled out to farm families to give Alaska a new and profitable home industry. The musk oxen grow fast, produce yearly in captivity, and give up to six pounds of qiviut per annum.

Eastern woolen mills are ready to underwrite the wool crop of the musk oxen, Teal said. Six pounds of wool per musk ox per year as against three ounces per cashmere goat! The idea has great possibilities if intelligently pursued, Teal declared.

What does Andy think about the possibility of musk oxen in our future?

"If they can help our economy, I'm for them," Andy said wisely. "I've learned never to pooh-pooh any innovation or development in four-legged farming.

"It wasn't long ago that the Alaska reindeer was supposed to be headed for extinction," he pointed out. "Today, with care and supervision, it's making a comeback. In the fall of the year you can get reindeer steaks, chops and roasts in markets throughout Alaska."

Whether it's musk oxen, or sheep, or pigs or beef cattle, the livestock industry is on the increase in the north country. Through I. M. C. Anderson's encouragement, it has a chance of becoming one of Alaska's most important agricultural businesses.

There are thousands of acres of land just waiting for ranchers and cattle to move in. But these ranchers must know ranching, and they must know cattle. What is more, they must be financially able to tide themselves over several years

of learning about Alaskan conditions and the Alaskan modes
of operation.

Andy says, "Don't sell Alaska short when it comes to the
meat and meat products business. I've seen a lot of growth
up here in the North in the last two decades. Lots of people
said you couldn't raise cattle in eastern Oregon and Montana,
either, but time proved them wrong. The future in Alaska for
four-legged farming is even brighter."

11

How to Retire at Forty-three

BERT AND LEAH STIMPLE HAVE STUCK TO THEIR guns for almost a quarter of a century to prove a principle. They have established that farming in the Tanana Valley around Fairbanks can be a profitable industry. They have also proved that they could retire at the age of forty-three.

Bert came to Alaska in 1936, a Minnesota-grown farm lad whose roots were deep in the soil. He liked the looks of the Tanana Valley, and decided that therein lay his destiny. He would stay and homestead.

In those days there weren't many persons interested in getting homesteads in Alaska from Uncle Sam. There was lots of land available and Bert didn't have to queue up to the land office counter to wait for a chance to look at the plats of open ground.

In fact he got the undivided attention of the land office manager who peered somewhat skeptically at what he saw over the top of the counter. The small, slight lad standing there looked more like a high school sophomore than a farmer about to carve an empire for himself out of the wilderness. He was five feet four inches tall and weighed exactly 118 pounds — including shoe pacs and oversized topcoat.

"Do you know anything about farming, son?" the kindly old gentleman asked. "Especially potato growing?"

"Well, what I didn't learn back on the farm in Minnesota I'm willing to learn from the University of Alaska — or from anybody else who wants to teach me," young Stimple said confidently. "I'm used to cold winters and I'm not afraid of hard work."

The manager took his map and pointed to a plat not too far from town. "There's some pretty good land open on the Farmers' Loop," he said thoughtfully. "You might just take a look at it, young man."

Bert walked the twelve miles of the Farmers' Loop, a road that had been brushed out to bring cordwood into town.

The 160 acres open were on the south slope of the hills that screen Fairbanks from the chill Arctic winds. It was heavily wooded with birch, willow and spruce. Bert climbed half a dozen trees to get a better view of the land. Most of it faced east and south, and these exposures would be freest of permafrost. The ground would thaw early in the season and remain unfrozen until the end of the growing season.

"I'll take it," Bert said to himself.

When the land office manager saw how determined Stimple was to get this homestead, he took a personal interest in the young man.

"I can't figure out what brought a young fellow like you way up here all alone," he said repeatedly.

"I told him it was a long story that went back to the depression," Bert related. "Pop had a farm and a good one, but he owed a note on it. During the Hoover boom the banker foreclosed on the farm and along with so many other 'indigents' of that period Pop and Ma and we four kids migrated to California. I was not quite sixteen at the time; it made a Democrat out of me!

"I finished high school and graduated from Santa Ana Junior College in 1935. For every job that was available there were about fifteen guys after it. They hired the bigger kids, and I could find nothing except piecework in the orchards. So I joined the CCC at thirty bucks a month, saved about two hundred and forty dollars, and burned my bridges behind me.

"In the spring of 1936 I rode a thirty-five-dollar motorcycle named Rosie to Seattle and then came steerage to Valdez," Bert went on. "As soon as Thompson Pass opened up, I putt-putted over the Richardson Highway to Fairbanks. I guess I came to Fairbanks because I'd heard more about it than anyplace else."

For Bert it proved to be a providential choice. With the advice and help of the land office manager he laid out a blueprint for his homestead. "Since I wasn't twenty-one until October, I 'squatted' on the land and began the buildings. I filed on the land on my twenty-first birthday, and the filing fee was sixteen dollars, a lot of money in those days."

Bert obtained title to his land three and one-half years later. "But it was a lot harder work than I ever dreamed of," he confided. "To make ends meet I went to work part-time in the Federal Building, first as janitor and then as post office clerk. I used what money I made to clear a little land, and by 1937 I had a few spuds in the stores."

By 1938 Bert had three acres cleared. "And by 1939 I no longer had to rent a horse," he chuckled. "I had bought a small tractor and a 1918 Model T Ford. The Ford cost twenty dollars.

"Luckily I'd also finished a pretty good log cabin, because

about this time two sisters I'd known in California came to Fairbanks to teach school. But before they got around to it, one of the girls had married a preacher, and Snukie had married *me*," Bert said.

"I used to tell her she'd never had it so good," Bert laughed, "but I'll bet there were times when Snukie wished she'd stuck to teaching. Not that she had much time to think about it. We farmed all day, and we both did janitorial work at night."

The Stimples became one of the outstanding farm couples in the Tanana Valley. Hard-working, friendly and community-minded, they made their log cabin a popular gathering place, and the teapot was always on for visitors. Snukie's coffee cake was superb.

Snukie, whose real name is Leah, weighed exactly seventy-eight pounds and measured four feet nine inches when she stood straight up. Despite her size, she turned a trick or two of her own and started raising tomatoes. Raised and ripened them out-of-doors, which people said was an impossibility so far north. In the fall she put $1200 in the bank from her tomato patch, and Bert said joshingly, "Gee, those tomatoes made my wife awfully hard to handle."

The Stimples got their first break in 1940. Always on the lookout for new merchandising ideas, they decided to sell their potatoes in attractive ten-pound mesh bags under their farm-brand name "Sprucehaven."

"With our Sprucehaven spuds we introduced the washed potato commercially to Fairbanks, much to the disgust of a few of the old-timers who preferred to sell ninety-five pounds of potatoes and about five pounds of the farm in each one hundred-pound sack," Bert remarked. "But it really paid off. We got a trip to California that winter."

Business was good. "We did so well on our potatoes —
and Snukie's tomatoes — that I thought I'd write a book
about 'How to Be a Successful Farmer in the Tanana Valley,'" Bert said.

"Then along came 1946. Just when we thought we had
her made, Alaska got its first attack of bacterial ringrot in
potatoes and wiped us out."

The Stimples' anticipated earnings shrank to zero and their
cash reserve dried up.

"We worked most of that year at Ladd Air Force Base to
pay off the indebtedness of that fatal harvest and to import
a new brand of Teton seed potatoes from Laramie, Wyoming," Bert recalled. "Those potatoes cost thirteen cents a
pound landed here, but we had no more ringrot because this
variety is resistant to it."

The spring of 1947 saw the Stimples planting their Teton
potatoes on twenty acres of a new 160-acre farm on the Steel
Creek Road, about ten miles northeast of Fairbanks. "We
sold Sprucehaven and decided to get up where we could
look out over the Tanana Valley," Bert said. "Our Green
Valley Farm was in an area known as Holy Hill, because
originally the preachers living here outnumbered the lay-
men. Since then most of the preachers have moved away, or
died, and the area is occasionally referred to as Sinners'
Gulch.

"That year we experimented with irrigation, the first in
the area," Bert explained. "We gave those Tetons better care
than you'd give a baby, watched them day and night. And
with practically twenty-four hours of daylight in June and
July, that's easy to do."

That first year, with irrigation, the Stimples averaged thirteen tons of potatoes to the acre. They celebrated by buying

more land, working harder, and rejuvenating their 1918 Ford.

"We got ourselves a new tractor and a new potato digger, and that cut down on our back-bending outdoor work," Bert related. "But what kept a lot of people from farming up here was having to pump their water by hand and light gasoline lanterns and drive ten miles to the nearest telephone. Not to mention the outdoor facilities and Sears, Roebuck catalogues."

It was 1951 before REA came to the Tanana Valley, "but it sure changed things in a hurry," Bert said. "As soon as the Golden Valley REA Association started generating, power lines started creeping out from town in all directions.

"More than any one thing, that 'juice' emancipated us farmers," Bert acknowledged. "We got lights, hot water, electric pumps, electric potato washers and electric washing machines.

"It wiped out our physical and mental isolation," he observed.

Other farmers started moving out the Stimples' way, and the Fairbanks School District established a bus route on the Steel Creek Road. The first bus was a sedan, and there were only four kids of school age. Six years later there were seventy. "However, the rate for the next few years will not increase so rapidly, as we now have television," Bert explained with a straight face.

With twenty-four-hour-a-day radio programs, some direct from the Outside, farmers can carry transistor radios with them in the fields or on their rounds in the barn so they can get the World Series and the college football games.

Additional lines are being strung into the Tanana Valley hinterlands to bring the "Pioneer Telephone Association" into farm houses. "Just think," Bert exulted, "we'll be able to talk to any place in the world right from Green Valley Farm!"

All these conveniences have brought a new type of farmer into the Tanana Valley. He is a married man with a young wife and a growing family. The old bachelors — the original Sourdoughs who moved out into the country to get away from it all, and the mechanics turned farmers — have left to subsist elsewhere.

The new settlers want to make money on the farm, and they want a good life to boot. They pull their own weight in the community and are giving farming in Alaska a good name, Bert said.

"The ones who are getting along the easiest and making the biggest success of farming are those who've come up here with money and experience," Bert pointed out. "They've taken agricultural courses in college, or they've worked on a farm, or maybe both. Otherwise they usually haven't lasted very long."

While many of the newcomers went in for dairying or truck farming, the Stimples stuck pretty much to potatoes. Today they own 280 acres in the Steel Creek area, of which 120 acres are cleared. Bert planted only forty acres of potatoes per year, rotating his fields on a three-year basis. The two fallow years he planted the other fields to peas and oats, and plowed them under as green manure.

In cooperation with the University of Alaska Experiment Station, Stimple has determined that maximum crop production can best be obtained by this three-year cycle, as the green manure gives the soil the humus and the tilth necessary for a bumper crop.

"We kept our potatoes under refrigeration twelve months

of the year," Bert said. "Stored at thirty-three degrees constant temperature, last year's potatoes were just as firm and marketable as the new crop."

Although Bert is an inveterate joker, he's also a practical man and a leader in the farmers' movement in Alaska. He helped to establish the Alaska Agricultural Loan Act which today has $450,000 available for farm loans in the new state. Bert also served faithfully on the Loan Board.

"The program has financed root cellars, barns, wells, land-clearing, machinery, livestock, seed and fertilizers," Bert recounted. "All four of the new Fairbanks dairymen used farm loans to help get started. Only one farm loan in all of Alaska has gone sour, and that was recovered, so there was no loss," he said proudly.

Bert was also instrumental in helping to sell the idea of potato grading laws in Alaska, and today all farmers marketing spuds to the public must have their crops inspected. Only U.S. No. 1 quality may be sold through retail outlets. Recently the Tanana Valley Farmers have affiliated with the Matanuska Valley Farmers Cooperating Association for grading, storing and merchandising their 3000 tons of potatoes annually.

Stimple pointed out one drawback to the merry cycle of farm profits in potatoes. The Tanana Valley is now growing just about the maximum tonnage of potatoes the local market can absorb. Any additional market will have to come from increased civilian families and increased military personnel on the bases or at DEW Line radar sites in the upper Arctic.

Over the years Bert and Leah won their premier position in the Fairbanks potato market by consistently highest quality and attractive packaging. They also had the lowest production cost for potatoes in the Tanana Valley.

"The way we grew potatoes, we had our cost figures down to the last decimal," he explained. "Seed, labor, insurance, depreciation, taxes, gas, utilities, packaging, refrigeration and selling — the total came to about three cents per pound.

"In June, July and August of 1957 we averaged eight cents a pound for our potatoes, and that isn't bad. If you'd like to see my books I'll be glad to show them to you. Internal Revenue looks at them so why shouldn't you?" Bert said with a twinkle.

With an average of eight to ten tons to the acre — and about forty acres per year — well, Bert and Leah Stimple retired from potato farming in 1958 at age forty-three.

And here is where our story should end.

But instead of getting into their 1918 Ford and driving off into the sunset, the Stimples visited around the valley and talked farming with their neighbors. "We've leased our acreage out to the younger generation," Bert explained, hiking up his galluses, "and we're going to take it easy. No more potatoes."

It wasn't long until Bert had talked with James Wilson, Commissioner of Agriculture for Alaska, and before Bert knew it he had accepted the job of Produce and Crop Inspector for the Fairbanks area.

"With all Bert's experience we couldn't let him sit around doing nothing," Jim explained. "He won't be just inspecting crops; he'll be helping the farmers and homesteaders over their hurdles and he'll be talking before civic clubs and farmers' meetings. This job will really be an 'avocation' for him — and there's no one who could do it better. Newcomers, especially, will benefit from his counsel."

In the past twenty years Stimple has been on every existing rural board: Farmers Co-op, REA, Farmers Home Administration, Alaska Soil Conservation Board, Territorial Loan Board, and the Fairbanks Sub-District Soil Conservation Board. He also has been the perennial farm industry representative on the Fairbanks Chamber of Commerce Board of Directors.

With this background, Bert has made it his business to know all the farmers in the vast Central district of Alaska. But he's quick to point out that it really isn't business, it's pleasure. "The rural folks, the homesteaders — they're the finest people in Alaska," he says with pride. And he makes their problems his problems.

Bert will assist farmers in planning their crops and their fields so there won't be an overproduction of potatoes and a scarcity of lettuce and cabbage. He's also working on higher prices for the potato growers. "The eight cent per pound potato is gone — at least temporarily," he said. "The potato market is disorganized and that makes the spud game at present very unattractive. But we think we can get it into the black again."

The potato farmers around Fairbanks rib Bert about his new job. "For twenty years you've been telling us how to plant our spuds and fertilize our crops. Now you're getting paid for talking!"

But Bert has a comeback. "You know, it took quite a while for people to realize that what I had to say was worth real money."

Young Stimple is most happy in his new work. "Snukie and I talked it over, and she is going to let me work with the farmers until I'm fifty and ready for a wheel chair. Then we're *really* going to retire and have a look at the smaller states."

Those who know the Stimples well don't think that Bert

and Leah will ever retire. "When you've put as much of yourself into a country as the Stimples have, you don't leave when it's on the threshold of its most exciting development," one of their close friends stated. "Even at fifty they'll be much too young and have too much to give Alaska to put themselves on the shelf."

Besides, Bert has become interested in a new facet to the agricultural picture around Fairbanks. Grain.

"People's diet habits are changing radically," Bert stated. "All these articles and books on eating your way to health are making Americans so conscious of vitamins and high proteins that they won't touch anything unless it's hepped up with A-B-Cs and all the minerals.

"And there's no better place to grow foods with higher nutrients than in Alaska," he pointed out. "The grains maturing in the Tanana Valley have the highest protein content of grains grown anywhere on the North American continent.

"These products, with a 'Grown in Alaska' label on them — and a big pitch as to their high protein, vitamin and mineral content — would be a natural for health food stores across the nation, as well as for the supermarkets."

Bert explained how some of the Minneapolis milling companies were interested in our grains way back in the '30s, and sent men to Fairbanks to study the long-daylight, short-growing-season cycle. The war killed the project, but lately several Outside companies are again expressing interest.

"If we can get Midwest capital to finance our wheat, oat and barley farms, think how it would boost our economy," Bert said. "There are thousands of acres of land that could be put under cultivation. We could also raise grain for cattle feeding. Barley gets a high yield up here. So does brome grass.

"This year the farmers up here are planting about two thousand acres in grain — an all-time high," Bert said enthusiastically. "And this past season, almost three hundred acres of brome grass were planted on *bottomland*. We used to think bottomland was no good because of the permafrost. But we've had some dry summers lately, and instead of the tall stand of grass drying up, we've saved our hay crops because of the moisture from the permafrost.

"You know, I think grain growing in the Tanana Valley could be a very profitable business — that is, if it were done right," Bert said with a sly look. "If we weren't going to retire when we reach fifty, Snukie and I might give it a fling."

Book Three

12

Keep Alaska Green—Send Tourists

THE BIGGEST MAN IN ALASKA'S POTENTIALLY BIG-gest industry is a fast-talking, boyish-looking fellow who has proved there's gold in them thar tourists. In less than fifteen years he has built up a big business on the premise that all Americans want to see Alaska and are willing to pay for the privilege.

Charles "Chuck" West is the kingpin of the Alaska tourist industry. At age forty-five he has acquired two oceangoing steamships, eight highway buses, a motel, a river steamer, two roadhouses and three travel agencies. He employs Eskimo hunters, ivory carvers, spielers, ticket sellers and Arctic dancing maidens.

He gives the American tourist the flavor of the old Sour-dough days — with innerspring mattresses and good food thrown in.

He has hit the jackpot with a formula that says every traveler should get at least a *taste* of everything he pictures Alaska to be.

"And that's a whopping big order," West conceded.

"It means a trip north on the Inside Passage — the eight-hundred-mile steamer route with beautiful scenery slipping by while you sit in a steamer chair, play shuffleboard, get sunburned, have a drink or play bridge with shipmates from California, Texas and New York.

"It means totem poles in the Panhandle — Mt. McKinley in the Interior — and Eskimoland in the Arctic," he said quickly. "And the Midnight Sun and gold dredges and king crab and muktuk.

"The tourists also want action, lots of it," Chuck emphasized. "Lots of things to see and do — excitement. We give it to them. We let them feel an iceberg. We give them a drink with ten-thousand-year-old glacier ice in it — and we get ourselves a pack of satisfied customers."

Chuck West is known all the way around the world as an entrepreneur in the travel business. In Madrid they speak of him as "The Eskimo Man." Since the advent of statehood, travel agents in the other states have started addressing him as "Mr. Alaska." Chuck grins, shows his white, even teeth, and mentally keeps ringing up the cash register.

Chuck is always in a hurry and keeps his associates out of breath with his feverish pace. "We Alaskans have got to get off the dime," he cries in semi-anguish. "Look. Maine — California — Bermuda — Hawaii — Mexico — they've all shown that the tourist industry is an artesian well of crisp green cabbage.

"And Alaska? It's got more to sell than any of these places. Its attractions are unlike any on the beaten travel routes. It's in a class by itself.

"All that you people from Ketchikan to Point Barrow have to do is supply the beds and I'll keep Alaska green with greenbacks — and tourists," he promised. "All you have to do is provide the type of accommodations that travelers are accustomed to having, and you've got yourself an inside pipeline to perpetual prosperity."

These accommodations, West contends, should cover a price range as wide as the American pocketbook. They should cater to Mrs. Park Avenue and also to the economy-minded schoolteacher who has exactly so many pennies to spend.

West is most generous with his philosophy of how to build a fat income in the tourist industry in Alaska. "It's simple," he says. "The more operators we have up here who give good service to the traveling public, the better publicity we'll get and the more tourists will want to come up and spend their money.

"Don't worry about treading on my toes," he laughs confidently. "I'll get my share."

West got into the tourist business by way of an airline job. He has always been able to see the dollar possibilities of any situation. Also he's never been deterred by any possibility of failure.

"I got that into my bones from flying the Hump during the war," he exclaimed.

Like most Alaskans, Chuck was born Outside. A native of Des Moines, Iowa, West contends that his parents took him to Los Angeles at the age of two to give him a better opportunity to develop his lung power. "I've been talking and selling ever since," he said with a quick smile.

After Hollywood High School and UCLA extension, West joined United Airlines in traffic and sales. In 1939 he became district sales manager of Western Airlines, and two years later was named their regional sales manager for Southern California, Nevada, and Arizona. He also learned to fly.

When Western Airlines became a contract flyer for the Army Transport Command, Chuck West, on request, became a fly-boy to chauffeur DC-3s and fighter planes to Alaska.

Chuck had a personal reason for wanting to go north. In Claremont, near Los Angeles, he had met Miss Marguerite Lee of Nome who was attending Scripps College. She was blond, a former "Miss Alaska" beauty contest winner, and Chuck had ideas concerning her future.

To this day, friends are still amazed at how frequently West got assigned to the Nome flight — and how regularly he seemed to be putting his feet under the mess table at the Lee Brothers gold dredge. Chuck never missed a bet or a meal.

West's skill at salesmanship paid off, and he and Marguerite were married in 1943 before he was due to go overseas. They now have five children — three girls and two boys — and Chuck is a proud and happy husband and father.

Chuck flew 153 missions over the Himalayas as a "Chinese Colonel" in the Flying Tigers. After that he knew he could do anything.

His first postwar job was flying the old Boeing 247-Ds for Wien Alaska Airlines, which had the contract between Fairbanks and Point Barrow for the Navy petroleum project.

But Chuck was too ambitious to be just an aerial jockey. When people asked him about flying into the mysterious Arctic, Chuck saw the dollar sign on far north tourist travel just as vividly as Sourdoughs saw the northern lights.

He sold the Wien brothers on a $75 one-day excursion from Fairbanks to Nome and Kotzebue, and he loaded the planes. To persuade Alaskans to visit the upper half of their territory — the unknown Arctic — he put on a weekly radio program in Fairbanks called "Wings Over the North."

In 1946 Chuck quit his job with Wien to start on his own. He contracted to act as ground crew and dispatcher for American Airlines, then a military contract carrier into

Alaska, and took care of their turn-arounds at Ladd Field, near Fairbanks.

One day Chuck heard a couple of workmen complaining about paying $149.50 to Pan American for a one-way fare from Fairbanks to Seattle. That was all he needed.

American Airlines and other contract planes were returning to the States empty. For a modest sum, Chuck made a deal with the operators to charter their planes on the return trip to the States. He started a hot advertising campaign and filled the planes at $100 per bucket seat.

This boosted the non-scheduled passenger business between Alaska and the States, and it started a bank account for Chuck West.

The old Napoleonic adage that a small man gains stature by getting on a horse applied in Chuck's case. He'd been operating out of a small cubbyhole in an old tin warehouse on a back street and he needed a "front." So he went to the late famous Captain Austin E. Lathrop, who owned the finest office frontage in Fairbanks.

"I've got a terrific selling idea, Cap," Chuck explained with his usual modesty. "But to put it over, I've got to get up on the sidewalk."

Cap listened to Chuck's persuasive proposal of establishing an airline ticket office on the mainstem of Fairbanks. Cap was impressed by the drive of this young man on the way up, and when Chuck walked out of the Lathrop Building he held a lease to the choicest office location on Second Avenue.

Construction workers often stood three deep in Chuck's new Arctic Alaska Travel Service office buying tickets for a bucket-seat ride to Seattle. They came on Saturdays and Sundays and until 10 o'clock at night.

West bought his first tailor-made suit that fall.

But the non-scheduled southbound passenger business was just one of Chuck's many ideas. He decided to revive the lucrative tourist industry which had been killed by World War II after being so painfully built up during the '20s and '30s.

As a self-appointed representative from Alaska, West went Outside in 1947 and attended the American Society of Travel Agents' convention. On sheer, youthful nerve he promised accommodations for all travelers who were sold Alaskan tours by members of the ASTA.

"I realized we didn't have hotel rooms to sleep many tourists, but I was determined to do something," Chuck reminisced. "I knew I didn't have to worry about Fairbanks. We had Mrs. Eva McGown, who handled the Chamber of Commerce Housing Bureau, and she knew every bed in town and when it was vacant.

"We had to house many tourists in private homes, but we made out. To say that some of the tourists were not overly thrilled with their accommodations is an understatement," Chuck confessed. "But nobody sued the company or took a potshot at me."

In conjunction with the Alaska Steamship Company, Chuck reopened the Gold Belt Tours to the Northland. Tourists went by steamer from Seattle to Seward, by Alaska Railroad to Anchorage, Mt. McKinley and Fairbanks, and by bus down the Richardson Highway to Valdez. One hundred and twenty-seven tourists made the trip that first year.

In 1947 Chuck expanded the tours in cooperation with Wien Alaska Airlines and flew tourists from Fairbanks to Nome and Kotzebue. He hired Eskimo dancers at Kotzebue to put on shows for the tourists, and started a new summer industry and income for the natives. On the side the natives sold their ivory carvings and curios to the tourists.

"On the return trip we flew our planes out over the Arctic Ocean, dipped over the Arctic Circle, and circled Little Diomede Island. On good days we flew right down the International Dateline, with Russian Big Diomede Island just off our starboard wing. The tourists loved it, but we wouldn't be able to do that today!" Chuck exclaimed.

Chuck crisscrossed the United States making radio talks and explaining the ABCs of Alaska tourist travel to ticket agents in major cities. He got promises of double the number of tourists he'd had before.

"But 1948 turned out to be a big construction boom year in the Interior," Chuck said, "and we couldn't even get accommodations in private homes for all the tourists. The situation was desperate so another fellow and I bought surplus army tents, put them up, and put in wooden floors. Whether they liked it or not (and most didn't) we took care of four hundred and fifty tourists in Fairbanks during the summer.

"In 1949 we really expanded," Chuck continued. "We added a small stern-wheeler sight-seeing boat run by Captain Jim Binkley and his charming wife Mary. This riverboat chugged down the Chena River into the Tanana to visit an Indian village complete with lots of kids, barking dogs and a squeaking fish wheel. Jim and Mary were wonderful hosts and the tourists loved their line of chatter and banter.

"We also put on sight-seeing busses to the huge gold dredges around Fairbanks," Chuck stated, "and we opened an Anchorage office of our Arctic Alaska Travel Service."

The next year Chuck built his own motel just outside Fairbanks, and he opened two travel offices in Seattle to handle Stateside travel promotion.

His business boomed. He became a wheel in the newly formed Alaska Visitors Association which was organized to put Alaska on the map as far as the traveling public was concerned.

The AVA was created by the 1951 Alaska territorial legislature, and is financed by public subscription of business firms and individuals with matching funds from the state government. The AVA carries on a national advertising campaign, supplies travel agencies with "Alaska Travel Kits," sends out a million folders per year on Alaska, and helps to improve tourist facilities in the Northland.

Since AVA started selling Alaska to Americans, tourist travel to the Northland has almost quadrupled. AVA headquarters in Juneau reported that 87,000 tourists visited the Northland in 1958.

In 1954 the Alaska tourist industry got a bad blow. The Alaska Steamship Company decided to quit the passenger business to Alaskan cities. Airplane competition and demands of the unions caused them to throw in the towel.

"The next year we almost went under," West admitted. "All the money we made during the good years went right down the drain. We couldn't sell enough tourists on round-trip airplane travel to Alaska to pay our office help."

West tried another tack. He bought four busses, painted them Alaska's colors of blue and gold, and sent tourists up over the highway. A long-time Alaskan, Everett Patton, took charge of this division, and regaled tourists with heroic tales of the territory they were covering. But highway travel called for still another selling job. The roadhouses along the Alaska Highway and the Richardson Highway simply had to be improved. The era of the outside john was over.

"Some of the roadhouse keepers kicked," Chuck stated, "but since they wanted our business they finally complied. In a couple of cases we almost had to advance the money for installing inside plumbing."

His business rocked along during 1955 and 1956. In 1957 he decided to take a plunge. As long as tourists wanted to go to Alaska by steamer, he'd get them a steamer. He took a deep financial breath and said, "Here goes everything."

West chartered a Canadian passenger steamer to operate between Vancouver, British Columbia, and the Panhandle ports of Southeastern Alaska. She carried 120 passengers, a crew of fifty, and was a fine cruise ship for the Inside Passage.

Chuck gussied up the ship, added entertainment, and did a rip-roaring season's business. Tourists had their choice of several combination tours. They could go north by ship, fly to the Interior and the Arctic and then fly home. Or they could fly north and come back by steamer. Or they could make the round trip by boat. The complete tours took fourteen days — or longer, if the traveler preferred.

The venture clicked, and Mr. West was again strumming Home Sweet Home on the cash register.

After going into a financial huddle with himself and some startled bankers, Chuck bought the Canadian ship, renamed it the S.S. *Glacier Queen*, painted it blue and gold and got ready for a banner 1958 season.

When he got a chance to buy a sister ship to the *Glacier Queen*, Chuck decided to go all the way. With everything he owned in the world signed up as security he bought this second ship, renamed her the S.S. *Yukon Star*. His Alaska

Cruise Lines, Ltd., owns the ships and his own marine department operates them.

With this new setup, West adopted a policy that many an Alaskan interested in catering to the tourist can bear in mind.

The tourist season in Alaska in years past has always extended from June 15 to September 1. It blossomed suddenly, rose to a peak, and died out in one downward swoop. But some of Alaska's sunniest weather is in April and May, and September is as vivid in fall coloring as is autumn in New England.

So West decided the first four trips of the *Glacier Queen* and *Yukon Star* in May would be "Thrift-Season Trips" — at 25 per cent off. The same applied to the September sailings.

West's latest investment is a 41-passenger pressurized Highway Traveler, complete with bathroom facilities, which runs between Whitehorse and Fairbanks on the Alaska Highway. This de luxe motor coach is one of the finest pieces of equipment on the road today. "By the time we got it in operation, it added up to almost a thousand dollars per passenger," Chuck stated.

Chuck gives a lot of the credit for his successful operations to a bit of advice Cap Lathrop gave him along with his first office space. "The key to a young man's success is surrounding himself with people of equal or better ability than his own," Cap told him, and Chuck has worked on this precept ever since.

"I'd never be free to wheel and deal in steamships and hotels if it weren't for key people like Jack Musiel in Seattle and Brad Phillips and Ken Friske in Alaska who keep our business running smoothly," Chuck stated. "Ten years ago my dad retired, but he got so interested in the tourist business that he's been a contact man and tour host for us ever since.

"What my organization has done in travel promotion and tour conducting in Alaska is open to anyone," Chuck said. "The future of the tourist industry in the Northland is limited only by the facilities that are available in the 49th state to take care of people with money to spend. You give people a good time and they'll be glad to pay for it.

"But you must give them value received," Chuck emphasized. "The day is over when visitors will put up with anything just because Alaska is a frontier. They want good beds, clean bathrooms, good food and service with a smile — in Alaska as well as any place else. If you don't produce, you're cutting your own financial throat.

"We've been terribly hampered by lack of enough first-class accommodations throughout the Northland," Chuck stated. "But with statehood a number of Outside investors have become interested, and some are already putting money into hotel and motel facilities in the 49th state. I'd say that in the next few years a dozen de luxe motels will be built along the Alaska Highway and on the major roads in Alaska.

"Since statehood, too, there has been a big upswing in the hunting and fishing business — trophy hunters who want to bag one each of everything that walks, flies or swims. They come to Alaska from all over the world," he said.

"Professional guides, who've been struggling for years to make ends meet, are now booking parties of trophy hunters months in advance," Chuck went on. "The guides are improving their hunting lodges, buying new planes, more horses, hiring hostlers, packers and camp assistants.

"Some of this de luxe sporting trade is hiring professional photographers like Steve and Phyllis McCutcheon of Anchorage to make films of their safaris for polar bear, walrus, moose, caribou, sheep, goat or brownie.

"Alaska really has no competitors for the unique tourist attractions it possesses," West stated emphatically. "There is room for many good operators in the tourist industry. This can be Alaska's biggest cash crop — year after year after year.

"Tourism is not an end in itself," West acknowledged. "It brings financial investment, and it brings financial stability. And I don't know a nicer business in this world for meeting lots of interesting people — and getting paid handsomely for doing it," said the most successful Alaskan in the travel business. "That's why we say, 'Keep Alaska Green — Send Tourists.'"

13

How Oil Came to Alaska

THE BIGGEST SINGLE OIL LEASE BOOM ON THE North American continent, which now covers more than forty million acres, was born at 3:38 P.M. on January 18, 1951.

At that precise minute Ben Gellenbeck of Tacoma handed to Chester McNally, adjudicator of the Anchorage Land Office, 225 applications for United States oil and gas leases in the Territory of Alaska, with accompanying certified checks totaling over $125,000.

"Mr. McNally," Ben smiled, "I represent the Northern Development Company of Tacoma, which is a partnership of William T. Foran, a geologist, and myself. We request that all these applications be regarded as a simultaneous filing."

McNally's eyes popped a bit as he lifted the stack and placed it on his desk.

Casually he inquired, "What area does this cover?"

"About a hundred and fifty miles along the Gulf of Alaska — from the mouth of the Copper River to Icy Bay. This filing contains better than half a million acres."

McNally looked up at Gellenbeck. Then a very broad grin spread across his face. "For months I've been wondering when somebody would wake up and find a way to file on this petroleum province," he said. "My congratulations, sir. *There is nobody ahead of you.*"

Only an oil scout, a lease broker or a land man for a petroleum company could appreciate the feeling of relief that came over Gellenbeck with that statement: "There is nobody ahead of you."

Since that historic filing, Alaska has become one of the hottest wildcat areas in the world. Almost half of Alaska's potential oil lands have been applied for or leased. Producing wells have been drilled. Operators from all over North America have joined the land play.

But before Alaska's petroleum past gets buried in the present, and everybody gets into the act, we should like to tell the story of "How Oil Came to Alaska."

This is the story of three men — a geologist, a lease man, and an attorney — and how they accomplished the "impossible" in opening up Alaska's potential oil reserves.

It starts in 1923 when a young petroleum geologist by the name of William T. Foran was sent north with a party to investigate the petroleum possibilities of the Arctic slope for the United States Geological Survey.

For years, rumors had trickled out from whalers and traders about the tar pits at Point Barrow and other spots along the Arctic rim. Early adventurers had chopped hunks out of the oil-soaked tundra and tossed them into their stoves where they burned like coal.

The reports that Bill Foran brought back to the U.S.G.S. were so encouraging that he was sent north again the following year. Foran did a remarkable job. Out of these explorations came the first authentic data that some day the Arctic region of Alaska might become an enormous oil-producing province.

Unfortunately, further Arctic explorations were killed by the Teapot Dome scandal. Congress became nauseated with the smell of oil, and U.S.G.S. appropriations for petroleum investigation in Alaska were cut off at the pockets. Bill Foran hired out to Standard of New Jersey and went to South America.

Foran won his spurs as a reconnaissance geologist in Bolivia and points south, but he never forgot Alaska. Some of the boys who had been up north used to sit around the camps below the equator and bull about Alaska. "We all wanted to go back," Bill said.

After eleven years in South America, Bill was given a change of scenery and went to Baghdad. Foran is a medium-sized Irishman who takes no one's word for anything — least of all petroleum geology. He did his own field work and is credited with one of the major discoveries in that area — the Ain Zalah Field in Iraq.

When Nazi agents caused unrest in the Iraq oilfields during World War II, and Arab outlaws shot non-Germans at so much per head, Bill miraculously escaped into the desert. He figured he'd live longer if he went back to the United States, and his company thought so too. For the next few years Bill worked for a subsidiary of Standard of New Jersey in the noncombatant zone of Los Angeles.

In 1943 Bill Foran got his wish to return to Alaska. Because of his early experience in the Northland, and the outstanding job he had done for U.S.G.S. in geologizing the Arctic, the Joint Chiefs of Staff put him in charge of a section of their Alaskan oil operations. In the uniform of a Navy lieutenant, Bill went back to the same area he had covered in 1923 and 1924. His title was Chief Geologist for the Technical Sub-Committee of the Army-Navy Fuel Oil Board for Alaska, and his job was to come up with the right answers to three questions:

(1) If our normal Middle East and South American sources of oil are cut off by war, what can we expect from Alaska?

(2) If we have a twenty-five-year war with Germany and Japan, can we quickly develop a source of oil in Alaska, and if so, where?

(3) If we have a fifty-year war, can we get a sustained supply of petroleum in Alaska, and if so, where?

As a wartime measure, all potential oil lands in the Territory were withdrawn from public entry and turned over to the Navy as nominal custodian.

More than a score of top-flight geologists were assigned to Foran's staff. He worked at a killing pace, and drove his team just as hard. Bill was tenacious and exacting, and he left nothing to chance. He checked every bit of data himself, and covered all of Alaska before he was satisfied his information was correct.

In just a year and a half after he was given his assignment — months ahead of his target date — Foran notified the Joint Chiefs that he was ready to give his report.

Before a star-studded session of high brass in Washington, including Secretary of the Navy James E. Forrestal, Bill outlined the geology of the Arctic slope area — Naval Petroleum Reserve No. 4 and beyond. He explained why the nearby Umiat and Gubik structures were right for oil and gas. He showed where to drill and why.

Bill had painted a petroleum geology map of the Territory on a roll of white kitchen oilcloth, and he unrolled it dramatically to show some startling statistics on Alaska's oil potential.

The assemblage was amazed by Foran's disclosure that Alaska had upwards of 100 million acres of potential oil lands. According to Bill, the Territory contained not just one large petroleum province — but a minimum of six likely areas.

In essence, Bill told his tense audience, "Naval Reserve No. 4 is for the long haul — the fifty-year war. But other areas in Alaska would lend themselves to quick development, as they are either on year-around ocean transportation or very close to it."

He pointed out a five-million-acre province along the Gulf of Alaska, which included Alaska's first oilfield at Katalla. Eighteen shallow wells were brought in in this area from 1902 to 1933, and over 150,000 barrels of oil were sold to nearby towns and canneries before a firebug destroyed the topping plant.

Bill emphasized that this coastal region had many known seeps, that the climate would permit year-around drilling, that transportation was no problem.

Foran's map indicated petroleum possibilities that had never before been suggested: the vast Bristol Bay basin, home of Alaska's lucrative red salmon industry; the wide, flat Yukon-Kuskokwim Delta country; the Copper River Basin; and several areas in Central Alaska stretching eastward beyond the Canadian border.

Foran's detailed analysis of the oil potentialities of Alaska, combined with the brilliance of his work, so impressed Secretary Forrestal that he wrote Lieutenant Foran a personal citation.

Bill returned to Point Barrow, and in the following months supervised the exploration work at Umiat which confirmed his prediction that oil in commercial quantities would be found in that structure. He also directed the explorations in the adjacent Gubik area which established the fact that a gas field of major importance awaited development.

In 1946, Foran returned to inactive status, and set up a consulting geology office in Fairbanks. Later Pet. 4 was shut down, after the Navy had expended $60,000,000 in establishing that the Arctic slope could some day be the tremendous producer Foran predicted.

In 1947, Bill and his wife shook the tundra from their shoes and moved to Tacoma, where he became a lecturer in geology at the College of Puget Sound.

After twenty-five years in the oil game, Bill had learned many things. One of them was "never tip your hand." A lot of oil scouts can read things in the flick of a finger, and Bill's hands were mighty steady.

Bill taught geology for two years. When he finally did tip his hand, his deal was already signed, sealed and delivered — and on the way to making Alaskan oil history.

As Bill explained it, "While we were living in Fairbanks back in 1947, the *Daily News-Miner* carried a little two-inch story with a Washington dateline which said that all potential oil lands in Alaska, except the area on the Arctic slope, were being returned to public entry. When I read that, I almost jumped out of my skin."

After doing the petroleum geology on all of Alaska for the Joint Chiefs during the war, nobody in the world had as much knowledge of the oil potentialities of Alaska as did Bill Foran.

"I had to get Outside at once to put my knowledge to work," Bill stated. "I needed a cover story, so I got myself a job teaching a geology class at the College of Puget Sound."

Bill took his ideas to Ben Gellenbeck, an independent oil

lease operator of Tacoma. Ben had been western district manager for Keystone Lubricating Company of Philadelphia for twenty years, and had traveled extensively in Alaska.

Both men knew the government's leasing terms were most unattractive to oil operators because of the acreage limitations — only 15,360 acres for any one company or individual. Conservation laws, adopted back in the early part of the century, had closed up the Territory's oil explorations tighter than a drum. In such a vast area as Alaska, 15,360 acres was a mere flyspeck. And what company wanted to spend millions on a flyspeck?

But Gellenbeck had an idea. He was, first of all, a land man and an experienced one. He came up with a method of "unitizing" blocks of land into an area large enough to interest prospective drillers.

Bill and Ben set up a partnership called the Northern Development Company, which would act with power of attorney for several hundred individual leaseholders. All the leases would be filed as one block, and all leaseholders would share alike in the profits should oil be found anywhere in the entire block.

"We decided to unitize over a million acres on the Gulf of Alaska from the Copper River to Icy Bay — a part of the area Bill recommended to the Joint Chiefs for ready exploration and development," Ben explained. "We worked for eighteen months doping out lease descriptions for hundreds of miles of land that was unsurveyed and not too accurately placed on the map. We were doing something that had never before been done on such a large scale.

"Then we had to draw up leaseholders' agreements, options and powers of attorney. After the paper work was done, we had to sell a lot of people on the idea of taking out U.S.

government oil leases in Alaska, and get them to agree to a unitized working pool," he stated.

Those were nerve-wracking months for Foran and Gellenbeck. They worked frantically, afraid that time was running out, afraid that someone else would devise a similar leasing strategy and beat them to the land office. Their selling had to be done quickly and quietly — in fact, they tried to keep it completely hush-hush so that some lease hound or oil company wouldn't find out about their deal and file a bunch of "snakes" right down the middle of the area they wanted.

Almost three years of strenuous, exacting work had been put in by Foran and Gellenbeck before the first of their paper work was ready. The filing of 225 applications in the Anchorage land office in 1951 represented the largest block of unitized acreage ever assembled in the history of the petroleum industry under the American flag.

Within the next few weeks the Northern Development Company filed more leases, and upped its holdings in the Katalla-Yakataga region to 1,080,000 acres.

Gellenbeck and Foran then set out to sell their lease holdings to an oil company for exploration and development.

"We got what amounted to the heave-ho," Gellenbeck stated. "None of the major oil companies would believe us when we told them we could get the Department of the Interior to approve a development contract for a million acres in Alaska.

"A petroleum attorney in Washington, D.C., who was considered the final authority on such matters, said it couldn't be done. As most of the big companies were his clients, they were looking out the window when we were looking for an operator.

"The companies agreed the geology was favorable, that

Alaska offered great promise for oil, but they were certain we could not get a block of that size approved."

Ben knew, however, that two unitized gas deals had been approved. This was after the Leasing Act had been amended to give the Secretary of the Interior the right "to approve large-scale developments without regard to acreage restrictions when it could be shown they were *in the common good or national interest.*"

Ben was sure this could be applied to oil as well as gas. He played his hunch, and did a lot of praying.

In 1953 Phillips Petroleum Company agreed to prospect and drill the vast area — *if* Foran and Gellenbeck could get the Secretary of the Interior to okay a development contract.

They called in a Washington attorney, Nathaniel Jeremiah Ely, who had been president of the Washington Administrative Bar Association, and gave him the pitch. Ely knew his way around Interior. He knew when to smile, when to kid, when to talk turkey and when to sell. On February 6, 1953, Secretary of the Interior Douglas McKay approved the development contract as "being in the national interest."

Phillips Petroleum paid the Northern Development Company and its 539 leaseholders half a million dollars as bonus consideration, and started work in Alaska.

Foran, Gellenbeck and associates, including Nathaniel Ely, then formed the Yakutat Development Company to file on another million acres farther down the Gulf of Alaska coastline. After approval by the Secretary of the Interior, development rights to this area were purchased in 1955 by Colorado Oil and Gas Corporation, in association with the Frankfort Oil Company. They started drilling at Yakutat, and were later joined in the venture by the Continental Oil Company.

In all, Foran, Gellenbeck and associates accounted for 1009 lease applications and filed on 2,280,000 acres of land in Alaska. Their ventures were the beginning of what many oil men feel will be one of the most important petroleum developments of all time.

Some eighty companies and associations — and better than five thousand individuals — have already filed on more than forty million acres of Alaska's potential oil lands. And we might well look forward to a continuance of the present leasing spree until all this vast acreage is covered, along with all the fringe areas.

Hollywood movie stars, speculators, wildcatters and the "little man" have all plunked down their money at the land office in hopes of becoming oil barons. Local Alaskan stock companies have tried wildcatting. Some soon learned that there wasn't enough local capital in Alaska to support wildcats so they went to the States, hired theaters and salesmen, put on shows and sold stock.

Unitized groups were formed. An Anchorage businessman, Harold Koslosky, organized the Koslosky Development Company, and his brother Jan, of Palmer, formed the Petroleum Development Company — leasing ventures of 200,000 acres each in the Bristol Bay basin. The Great Western Development Company, headed by long-time businessman Roy Ferguson of Fairbanks, filed in the same area.

The biggest hurdle to oil leasing in Alaska was removed in 1954 when the Federal Mineral Leasing Act was changed to allow an individual, association or corporation to own 100,000 acres of federal oil and gas leases, and at the same time to hold options on an additional 200,000 acres.

With this change in regulations, interest in Alaska leasing started to skyrocket. The line formed to the right in the land office, and large chunks of potential oil-bearing acreage were grabbed up.

In the summer of 1957, all hell broke loose. Richfield hit commercial production on its first wildcat well on the Kenai Peninsula, just forty airline miles from Anchorage, and the town went mad. The well flowed at the rate of 900 barrels a day, and applications poured into the land office like a river on a rampage.

Lease applications rose to a record high of 390 in one day in the Anchorage office alone, and personnel fell weeks behind in their processing.

To top its first discovery, Richfield, in conjunction with Standard Oil of California, brought in a second producing well just a few miles from the first.

Considering that the average on wildcat drilling is nine dry holes to one producer — and that prior to the important discovery of the Leduc field west of Edmonton, Imperial Oil spent $23,000,000 drilling 133 consecutive dry holes — two producers out of two wildcats drilled on the Kenai was something of a miracle.

The oil fever flamed high in the Interior and into the Arctic. When four million acres east of the Gubik gas and oil structure in the Arctic were opened for non-competitive filing in the fall of 1958, there were 7406 lease offers filed in the Fairbanks Land Office for the 1320 parcels of land available. One man alone dropped in almost three thousand applications.

The drawing of lucky winners for this vast acreage took three days. A theater was hired for the performance, and land men for the big companies, lease hounds and individuals from throughout the Union converged on Fairbanks.

Today giant-sized rotary rigs are drilling deep on the

Alaska Peninsula, in the Matanuska Valley, in Bristol Bay, in the Kenai and along the Gulf of Alaska. Plans for additional wildcat wells are being projected in other parts of the vast new state as geologic and seismic work indicate the presence of structures which might contain commercial oil.

"A strike in another area of Alaska will start a boom that will make the present activities look like a kindergarten picnic," stated an official of the U.S.G.S. And when that happy event occurs, many experienced oil men have predicted that Anchorage could well become a second Tulsa.

What has been the impact of this beginning of an oil industry?

More than two hundred new families directly connected with oil companies in exploration and development have already come to Alaska. In Anchorage alone these newcomers have dried up the real estate market on better-type homes. The Petroleum Club of Anchorage grew in one year from a luncheon table of scouts and company representatives to a membership of 122. Fully three-quarters of the members have come to Alaska from other states.

Service industries catering to the oil business are locating in Anchorage, and a full galaxy will be here just as soon as more wildcatters drill holes and find commercial production.

What will oil mean to the future of Alaska? Many feel that it will be Alaska's greatest money crop. Rumors of new rigs, new land deals, new operating agreements, new companies and new drilling outfits circulate up and down the Alaskan scene every day.

As every oil man knows, oil is where you find it. But as far as the petroleum industry is concerned, $100,000,000 is now earmarked for exploration and drilling to find commercial oil in the hills and valleys of the 49th state.

No man is surer that they will strike — and strike big — than Bill Foran. As Ben Gellenbeck said, "Bill has never wavered in his belief that the oil potential of Alaska is tremendous. I have no doubt that his faith will be confirmed. When those new strikes come in, the citizens of Alaska will tip their hats to William T. Foran. It was his vision and knowledge that started the ball rolling to bring big-time oil to Alaska."

14

A Formula for a Fortune in Mining

No visitor to Alaska feels that his trip is complete until he has had a chance to pan for gold. And we old-timers in the country still get excited when we wash out a few colors in a rippling mountain stream.

There is a tremendous thrill to walking into the noisy, splashing creek, shoveling down a foot or so, filling a pan, washing the pebbles and sand out carefully, and finding three or four yellow flakes in the bottom. Eureka! The world is ours! We have struck gold in Alaska!

Then we dig again. A little more feverishly this time. We wash out just as carefully. But what went wrong? No colors at all! Hey, this ain't fair!

That's gold for you. As fickle as a maiden's kiss. You may go in pursuit of gold for a lifetime and never fill your poke. You may find a hot prospect and work yourself into a lather. But after a year's courting of the elusive treasure, you are sadder but no wiser. You'll surely hit it next year!

It is this hope in men's hearts — the inner conviction that their luck is in the next shovelful, the next foot of tunneling, the next outcrop — that keeps them prospecting.

But even if they discover a hidden bonanza, prospectors in today's world of inflationary values might have a hard time striking it rich. The position of gold on the American market has sent many an Alaskan gold seeker scurrying for a military construction job.

Where fifty years ago thousands of prospectors swarmed over Alaska's hills and valleys, only a handful of hopefuls still trek into the mountains every spring to look for their fortunes until the freeze-up drives them back to their cabins in the fall.

Today there are not a dozen gold mines operating in Alaska. Some of the small mines now being worked are good for better than day wages for their operators during the summer. But their number is dwindling.

"Gold mining is suffering from an acute attack of economics," stated William A. O'Neill, a consulting mining engineer who has had thirty years of mining experience in Alaska. "The costs are too high and the profits are too low. Everything has gone up except the price of gold.

"There's still lots of gold in Alaska, but the big operators aren't interested in marginal claims and high operating costs," Bill explained. "Many of them have gone to South America, Africa and Asia where they can get huge concessions and their labor costs are negligible."

If the gold senators in the United States Congress have their way, the price of gold in the United States will go to $70 per ounce, and open trading on the world market will be allowed.

Should the government hike the price of gold, the picture would change overnight, Bill pointed out. There would be a wild stampede to open marginal ground — just as there was back in 1933 when F.D.R. raised the price of gold from $20.67 to $35 an ounce.

"Incidentally, there are lots of people buying raw gold

from the mines today on just the hunch that the price will go up," O'Neill said. "They are paying on the basis of thirty-five dollars per ounce and stashing it away. They're gambling that gold will go to seventy dollars or more per ounce within the next five years. If it does, they will have made a sizable profit."

And for the same reason that many people make a killing on the stock market by getting into the game when the prices are down, this could be a good gambling time to get into the gold mining game in Alaska.

"But not if you know nothing about mining or about Alaska," Bill said emphatically. "Or if you are broke! Prospecting is expensive work, and mining your claim, if you find colors, costs nothing but money.

"The old Alaskan prospector gets along by himself because he knows his way around the hills, knows the climate, and can live pretty much off the land because he's been doing it for twenty-five to thirty years," he said. "Most newcomers aren't so lucky. Every year Alaskans have to go out and search for Cheechako prospectors who disappear into the wilderness. Usually the first anyone even knows about such a disappearance is when a man's relatives write from New Jersey or Ohio inquiring about him."

In both placer and hard-rock mining Bill knows whereof he speaks. He's spent over half his life in the mining game in the north country. At fourteen he went to work during summer vacations in the Chititu Gold Mine in the Copper River country above Cordova, operating a Swedish dragline on a placer property. A Swedish dragline, Bill explained, is a long-handled shovel using muscles for machinery.

At eighteen he was foreman of this big hydraulic property

that washed gold out of the gravel. But he decided if he were to get any further in the mining game he'd better go to college and round out his mining education.

He was graduated from the University of Alaska, class of '34, with a degree of Bachelor of Science in mining geology. In 1948 he was appointed a regent of the university, and today is vice-president of the board.

Bill has been a drill panner, hydraulic foreman, field engineer in charge of property examinations, and assistant manager of a large mining company. In 1947 he opened his own consulting office in Anchorage.

On his trips out into the hills, Bill can travel like a mountain goat. It is an education to go with him. You not only learn what you should be looking *for*, but you learn what you are looking *at*.

Old-timers who jealously guard a secret prospect or a quartz stringer or a bench lode trust Bill. He's one of them.

In the course of his business, Bill has answered hundreds of inquiries from people who want to come to Alaska and make a fortune in mining.

"If you have had a mining education, or a varied experience in mining in the other states or in foreign countries, you have a head start and a better chance up here," Bill explained.

"If you don't know one rock from another, and you're still determined to prospect, there is one way you can get a basic education in a hurry.

"The University of Alaska has a mining extension prospecting course tailor-made for anyone who wants a comprehensive capsule education in geology, mineralogy and the latest geochemical techniques," Bill stated. "The nine-week course,

which is given in towns, cities and military bases throughout Alaska, also features lectures on placer and lode mining
methods and mining law.

"Upon completion of the course you get a certificate —
but no guarantee that you'll discover a million-dollar pay-
streak," he observed.

It produces a lot of hopefuls, however. More than ten
thousand Alaskans — about one-fourth women — have taken
the course in recent years. Even if you don't invade the
hinterland with a prospector's pick and sample bags, you'll
have a better understanding of the type of terrain you're
looking at when you drive through Alaska's mountain ranges
or follow her streams.

"My suggestion to a Cheechako, after he has finished his
mining course, is to tie up with an old-time prospector who
knows the hills and how to take care of himself in the wilds,"
Bill advised. "Even though you may have your university
sheepskin, you can learn a lot from these old-timers.

"One thing you'll learn fast is that you don't find gold — or
any other mineral — right out in plain sight," O'Neill explained. "Most of Alaska's terrain is covered by dense forest
or heavy brush or thick tundra. You have to dig and scrape
to get a look at what the country is made of. Until you get
below the mantle of vegetation you can't do much prospecting."

If you're serious about prospecting in the far north, there
are literally hundreds of mining and geology reports on
Alaska, which will give you a background knowledge of the
country, available in libraries throughout the United States.
The State of Alaska Department of Mines in Juneau has
many reports and professional papers which will give you
years of experience to draw on, and the U.S. Geological

Survey has issued scores of reports on Alaskan minerals and geology.

"We get a lot of requests from people all over the country who want to get a job with a mining company, and maybe do some prospecting for themselves on the side," Bill said. "But I'm never very encouraging. I have to tell them that the only big mining operator left in Alaska is the U.S. Smelting, Refining and Mining Company, which operates gold dredges in the Nome and Fairbanks areas. This company is cutting down on its manpower because of high costs and diminishing returns.

"There are a few smaller going concerns like the Strandberg Brothers who mine in several locations, including the Manley Hot Springs area," he continued. "They employ around forty workers during the summer season, but they usually have a waiting list for jobs."

Bill, who has mined literally millions of dollars in nuggets and dust for some of the biggest gold mining companies in Alaska, feels that there is a definite place in Alaska for prospectors — lots of them.

"But before a prospector spends months on a hillside or out on the tundra he needs an incentive — a good gambling chance — that he'll be able to develop his million-dollar property, or that he'll be able to sell it to a well-financed operator. The prospector needs a sort of financial midwife to see him through the period from discovery to sale.

"For instance," Bill explained, "suppose you're a young fellow out in the hills and you've found some powerful good shows. You're all excited and you write to a big company and feel it won't be long until you're a millionaire. But what happens? You get back a form letter asking, 'How many tons of ore have you blocked out at present?'

"Well, you know you haven't even *one* ton blocked out. All you have is a vein on the side of a mountain. You've traced it for maybe five hundred feet. You've taken samples and had them assayed at the Alaska Department of Mines for free.

"All you have is a hopeful showing — a completely raw prospect. You can't go farther because you haven't got the money to pay for diamond drilling, for trenching the mountainside, or for a bulldozer to get up there and tear away the trees and overburden so that the hard-rock can be examined.

"And if you're like most young prospectors, your chances of getting that type of financing are nil," Bill said simply.

Bill then went on quietly and slowly. "Here is the formula for building that fortune in mining in Alaska: Alaskan exploration companies must be organized to bridge the financial gap between the prospector and the big operator. With a million dollars or more of expendable capital, the exploration company could take over where the prospector is forced to leave off.

"The exploration company would examine the outcrop, exposure, vein or hole in the ground, and, if it looked promising, would gamble whatever was necessary — a box of dynamite or a hundred thousand dollars — to find out whether the prospector's find would make a mine, or whether it's just a flash in the pan.

"If the property looks good," Bill went on, "the exploration company would be in a position to finance the mine's production, or to sell the mine. The prospector would get a percentage for his find, the exploration company would get a percentage for the risk it took, and Alaska would get a new business, revenue and payroll.

"When and if such exploration companies come into Alaska, literally hundreds of showings would pop up for them to investigate," Bill stated. "Old-timers would come out of the hills with whispered requests to look at their 'secret mines.' New prospectors would be encouraged to get out into the hinterland and make new finds. It would not be very long before Alaska would be on the way back as an important mining state of the Union."

O'Neill went on to explain that, while Alaska has not a single exploration company ready, willing and able to operate on this philosophy, Canada has many which have made splendid successes of taking a gambler's chance. Great ore bodies have been found on the other side of the border, following up on leads of prospectors who have brought in or mailed in a sack of samples they have knocked off an exposure in a canyon or on a cliff. Both the companies and the prospectors have made money.

This explanation by engineer O'Neill may be over-simplified, but when you consider that the mineral wealth of our neighbor to the east has been expanded by exciting new discoveries, while Alaska's has gone steadily downhill, his answer makes sense. After all, the fact that there is an imaginary line running between Canada and Alaska does not mean that all minerals and metals stop at this man-made border.

"Every state in the Union has mineral wealth of one kind or another," Bill remarked. "And seeing as Alaska is one fifth the size of the old 48 states combined, it's logical to assume that we have a good share of our country's metals and minerals."

There are known prospects of most of the strategic metals in Alaska. In the past two years two important discoveries of iron have been made in the new state. Both deposits have indications that they will be enormous.

One of these deposits was found by petroleum geologists flying with magnetometers to map possible oil structures. When they approached this iron deposit, hidden under the soggy tundra, their instruments went crazy. A planeload of iron experts from the Mesabi Range was flown in secretly to evaluate the deposit and stake it properly.

Bill O'Neill went on to analyze Alaska's mineral wealth. He pointed out that, with the drift of United States population constantly westward, the arrival of a major steel industry on the Pacific coast is not too far away. When that happens, the vast iron deposits of the Panhandle and South-central Alaska will enter the economic picture. The mountain range of magnetite at Klukwan, near Haines, which is said to be one of the largest deposits of iron ore on the continent, will then come to life. Scuttlebutt says that active mining of this deposit, owned by a subsidiary of U.S. Steel, will start in two years. It is still too early to tell whether the discovery of natural gas at Yakutat 125 miles away could turn Haines into a big smelter town.

Copper is a commodity always sought after by industry. Though the famed Kennecott Copper mines near Cordova played out in 1938 after producing $200,000,000 in copper, there are important prospects of this metal elsewhere in the 49th state. Nickel, mercury and tungsten are high on the priority list, and are known to exist in several regions in Alaska. There is one operating mercury mine — the Red Devil — near Sleetmute on the Kuskokwim River, which was bought by a Canadian syndicate a few years ago.

With the arrival of the petroleum industry in Alaska, a commercial deposit of barite or bentonite — thousands of tons of which are used in drilling oil wells — would be a profitable find.

And if some prospector finds a large deposit of vermiculite — widely used as house insulation — he will be able to walk through a field of Cadillacs in his bare feet. Insulation is a much-needed product for all building in Alaska. As population increases, and thousands of new homes and buildings are constructed, the demand for insulation will increase. At present, all insulation is shipped in from the Outside, and a home-grown insulation industry would have the freight rate from Seattle to Alaska as a protective tariff.

At present there is no brick factory operating in all of Alaska. Yet the proper clays are to be found in many localities. Ordinary chimney brick, the commonest product of the kiln, must be shipped in. It costs fifty-five cents per brick retail when it arrives in the growing city of Fairbanks.

Will Alaska have a cement plant soon? No one can answer that question. But the finding of a suitable limestone deposit near the major markets of the 49th state may provide the answer. Today all cement — thousands of tons of it — is transported by sea in bulk to hoppers at Seward, Anchorage and Fairbanks.

Long-fiber asbestos is now mined in several locations in the Canadian northland, not far from the Alaskan border. Perhaps it will be found on the American side of the line, also, to add to the economy of our new state.

Bill O'Neill says that there will be three large markets for Alaskan minerals and metals when they are developed into commercial ventures.

One market will be the million people who will be Alaskans within the next twenty years. Another will be the processing plants on the west coast, to whom we will supply raw materials for heavy industry. A third market will be Japan and the Far East. Alaska is 1500 miles closer to the awakening Asian market than is Seattle. This nautical distance can sell prosperity to Alaska.

The new state will do well to devise ways to help the prospector in his search for mineral wealth. But of this we may be sure: as the need for new sources of minerals and metals in our world expands, the vast reaches of Alaska will be more completely studied by geologists and mining men.

The plan outlined by Bill O'Neill for adequately financed development companies in Alaska could well make mining history in the Northland. Prospectors will make new discoveries in the hills and valleys that today we walk over, not realizing the deposits that are there.

And when that happens, more than one Alaskan will exclaim in mortal anguish, when he hears that someone has discovered a million-dollar mine of beryllium, vanadium or tantalite:

"To think that I walked over that mountain a dozen times — with a million dollars under my feet — and all I was looking for was a moose!"

15

The Industry Nobody Knows

A HUNDRED-MILLION-DOLLAR INDUSTRY HAS IN-
filtrated Alaska in the past few years. It has been one of the
well-kept secrets of the Northland, and not one Alaskan in a
hundred knows a thing about it except the initials which
make up its name. The DEW Line was born a mystery and is
likely to remain so.

A few years ago the military bundled up a bunch of newspaper reporters and flew them north for a long, chilly look
at our first line of defense. They got the full treatment, from
the top of the DEW Line's busy electronic brain to all its
pips and blips and its human components.

When they got back to their typewriters, these same news-
men wrote by-line accounts of the brilliant display of the
northern lights, the wild winds that screech by at 100 mph,
and how the boys from their home state were making out in
the Arctic.

"We learned early in the game that we could see all, hear
all, and tell nothing," one reporter confided. "When we saw
what was happening up there in the icy boondocks, we understood why.

"Standing on the edge of the Arctic Ocean, with nothing
in any direction but snow and ice and more of the goddam

stuff, we got a good healthy respect for the men who were running our polar defenses.

"Here we were, looking out over the Arctic waste, wondering what the big Russian bear was doing. We'd been briefed enough to know that Red scientists were turning out some devastating bombs and missiles that could come hurtling toward us at any split second. To save our own skins, not one of us would have written a word that was 'classified' about the DEW Line.

"After all, this line is our answer to whatever Ivanovich on the other side of the Pole decides to dish out," he stated. "It's just what the name says — a Distant Early Warning Line. This line stretches three thousand miles across the top of the free Arctic like an invisible wall. It's a vast network of radar installations that picks up all flying objects on its screens and 'beeps' a warning to the nation.

"Because of this line, we may have four to six hours' notice to get our own jets or missiles into combat," he continued. "It'll be a hell of a nightmare when they connect, but it'd be a lot worse if they got through to us with nuclear bombs and eliminated a large chunk of our population.

"The DEW Line is really an 'electronics genie,' " he said. "It picks up an approaching object with pips on the screen and warning beeps. A guy in the Arctic sees the pips, hears the beeps, and talks into his mike on a direct hookup with the Continental Air Defense Command in Colorado Springs. If the beeps are unfriendly — whammo! Intercepters will be in the air and on their way toward the enemy!"

This is the DEW Line simplified down to the fourth grade. Actually, nothing about the DEW Line is simple, not even its beginning.

The DEW Line is a product of our jet age. In these days of long-range bombers and guided missiles, the shortest distance between our potential enemy and ourselves is "right over the top."

Until recently, the snow and ice of the polar region had been a forbidding barrier to aggression. Aircraft couldn't traverse the long distances over the Pole without refueling. As late as 1949 the Defense Department proposed that Seattle's all-important Boeing bomber plant be moved to the heart of Kansas where it would be "safe" from enemy attack.

To that plan, Governor Ernest Gruening of Alaska offered a counterproposal: adopt a "polar preparedness" program instead of a "retreat" program. He suggested a top-of-the-continent warning system of some kind to alert the nation in case of attack.

Others agreed with his thinking. And with the manufacture of longer-range jet planes, and missiles that streaked through the heavens, the whole polar concept changed.

This new concept was the genesis of the DEW Line. For security reasons, only part of the story can be told. Officials can't be quoted. Sites can't be pinpointed. Any description of equipment and operation is taboo. Only authorized persons are allowed to visit its far-flung installations, and only general information filters out about its scientific operations.

Even its conception was secret. Early in 1952, the military called together at the Massachusetts Institute of Technology some of the country's leading scientific experts, and mysteriously dubbed them the "Summer Study Group."

Only they and the Pentagon knew why they were there. Into their laps had been dumped the problem of how to originate, build and operate a hoped-for enemy-proof defense warning system across the top of the world. These scientists were facing one of the greatest challenges of our age — one which could mean their own survival!

Where to begin? The problem was new in the field of electronics. It was top secret. And time was of the essence. The developments in radar had been advancing at such speed that it was a foregone conclusion that the warning system would be some adaptation of this new science.

The experts attacked the problem with true scientific zeal. The warning system would be in a completely new geographic area. How would it work at 60 below — and in a 100-mile wind? There was no textbook, no precedent on which to draw.

Through the hot, humid summer months the scientists sweated out designs for equipment to be used in the icy Arctic winters. On their drawing boards emerged a system of scanning stations to detect the approach of enemy planes and missiles. They drafted a method of shooting a continuous signal from the stations to a nerve center in the States.

These men put in endless hours devising their electronics equipment. They designed and redesigned; they built and rebuilt. They lived with their problem for months on end.

Finally came time to build a prototype station and see how the experiment would work out. Western Electric Company, a part of the far-reaching Bell System, was picked to do the job. In the quiet farming community of Streator, Illinois, about ninety miles southwest of Chicago, the first Arctic-type radar dome and necessary buildings and equipment were built and put into operation. In this tall corn country the men went about their work with a casualness that allayed suspicion. Under the guidance of the late Vern Bagnell (Bagnell Bay, near Point Barrow, is named for him), the bugs were worked out of the design of the operating units.

At the same time, other equipment was being tested under more frigid conditions. On Alaska's Barter Island, at the top of the continent near the Canadian border, Western Electric's electronic equipment got a de luxe taste of the polar weather that had knocked previous radar operations out of commission: violent summer electrical storms, biting winter gales that ripped off antennas, and the disturbances that accompanied the northern lights. But the scientists had done their work well. After a few revisions and adjustments, the DEW Line passed its tests with flying colors.

In December, 1952, the experimental line was ready to trek north.

The first links in the radar chain were built from Alaska's Point Barrow to Barter Island. To carry the system farther east, the United States made a treaty with Canada to locate, construct and operate scanning stations from the mouth of the Mackenzie River to the eastern shore of Baffin Island.

Along the ice-packed rim of the Arctic Ocean sharp-eyed, parka-clad pilots dipped their planes perilously low to search out possible station sites. They carried emergency equipment and survival gear — for the route they covered was so vast and lonesome that precious few Eskimos had ever passed that way.

All the way from Barrow to the Canadian border the coastline was one long, low beach. But farther eastward in the Canadian Arctic pre-Cambrian mountains rise sheer from the sea. DEW Line sites were laid out from one foot above sea level to 4000 feet atop near-vertical cliffs.

The first men to occupy some of these isolated sites were

paradropped. So were their tents, food, equipment, survey-ing instruments, extra clothing and walkie-talkies. Once the technicians had calibrated and evaluated the sites from the ground, C-124s paradropped snow rotaries and tractors. More men and equipment floated out of the skies beneath vari-colored parachutes. They set to work making runways so more men and equipment could be brought in.

Eight thousand men, 200,000 tons of cargo and $400,000,-000 built the 3000-mile Distant Early Warning Line across the northern rim of North America in 1955 and 1956. The western end of the line was at Alaska's Cape Lisburne — the eastern terminus was at Canada's Baffin Island.

The men who worked out logistics problems for the big pushes in World War II had nothing on the DEW Line boys. No recital here could ever convey the unprecedented and stupendous job of subcontracting for all the specialized equipment, machinery, spare parts, prefab units, lumber and thumbtacks needed for the 1955-1956 building program. Over sixty thousand suborders were let in different parts of the United States, with the delivery date for every part an absolute deadline.

A gigantic Arctic sea lift of heterogeneous naval equipment — all loaded to the gunwales — sailed north: big ships, little ships, LSTs, Victory Ships, tugs, icebreakers, repair vessels and other assorted floating craft. More than a hundred Navy ships unloaded men and supplies along the Arctic coast in the few weeks the ice pack moved away from shore.

The air armada which flew personnel and more supplies to sites in the remote Arctic was just as incongruous. New pilots, old pilots, veteran bush flyers and Cheechako fly-boys who had hardly seen snow before took off for the great white yonder in as many varieties of planes. They ran into blizzards which blanked out the runways; they flew in white-outs, when the land, sea and sky all looked one color — white — and there was no way of telling where one left off and the other began. They flew in 50 below and on days when they could hardly get off the ground at all.

There were accidents. Planes crashed. Ships were damaged by ice. But casualties were surprisingly few compared to the pressures and the size of the undertaking.

When the warning system was first planned, scientists decided World War III would be everybody's war. There would be no noncombatants. So the DEW Line was designed for civilian operation, releasing military personnel for active duty.

Civilian operators were being recruited for service, screened for security and trained for specific duties when word came from Washington that the entire DEW Line had to be in operation by the end of 1956!

Federal Electric Company, the service subsidiary of International Telephone and Telegraph Corporation, took over a crash training program. They recruited supervisors from within their own parent organization and flew the technicians — all trained in multiple jobs for operation of the stations — to the Arctic. By the end of the year every station was fully manned and operating efficiently. The deadline to protect America had been met!

Vice-Admiral Richard H. Cruzen (ret.) was the Federal Electric project manager of the DEW Line. This well-known Navy personality served in the North American Arctic during World War II, and was also operations officer for Admiral Byrd's Antarctic expeditions.

On the shoulders of assistant manager Myron Bakst, a tall, soft-spoken man from New Jersey, and an inspired staff, fell the detail of perfecting a smooth sequence from the first step, through the planning, subcontracting, and efficient manning and operating of the completed stations.

More than six hundred highly trained DEW Line employees are now in the Arctic, manning the scanners and performing all the duties of operating our vital defense system. The DEW Line hires electronics experts and mechanics, cooks and cat drivers — and traveling physicians, dentists and chaplains who make a continuous circuit of the radar sites. Employees are all men. Their average age is twenty-eight. And about half of them are married.

There is no racial discrimination on the DEW Line, and East and West and North and South work side by side and break bread together. Eskimos get equal pay for equal work with other employees.

The Eskimos make phenomenal mechanics and are among the best workers in their field. "They are loyal and dependable and have a perseverance that won't let them give up on any problem," one station manager said. "Their shy manners and their quick smiles and big sense of humor make them very popular with other workers.

"A lot of these natives fell in love with the white man's way of life when they worked on the Naval Petroleum Reserve, and, believe me, they're glad to be back," he said. "They found it awfully tough to subsist on blubber and muktuk between jobs."

DEW Line employees are so important to the defense of our hemisphere that every effort is made to see that they live well. They eat the best mess on the market, relax in well-equipped recreation rooms, listen to hi-fi and watch the latest movies.

Their quarters are warm and pleasantly decorated. Scientists, technicians, workmen and chefs set up shop and house-keeping in a series of module unit buildings, insulated and abutted in one long, compact line. The buildings contain dormitories, dining rooms, technical laboratories, laundries and hobby lobbies, and men can wander up and down from one unit to the other without poking their noses into the Arctic winter.

These unit buildings were turned out on an assembly-line basis in heated factories on the shore of the Arctic Ocean, and cat trains hauled them hundreds of miles to sites across the frozen tundra. Units are heated from waste heat of diesel generators and electronic equipment, which reduces the fire hazard in a country where tinder-dry buildings could be razed in minutes with the help of a few Arctic gusts.

From the air, these camps appear like dreary little oases clinging to isolated, wind-swept spots on the northern horizon. One employee wrote home that "A DEW Line site looks like nothing else in the world except another DEW Line site. The architecture is Early Arctic, circa 1955, characterized by the long, lean look of a squared-off Pullman train."

Three airlines service the DEW Line, bringing supplies, fresh food, replacement parts, mail and rotating personnel. Crisp green celery and milk fresh from the Matanuska Valley can do a lot to raise the morale of men living in a land where the sea is frozen ten to eleven months out of the year, and the winter moon is overhead most of the day.

It is only during the short, miraculous Arctic summer that the camps break free from the ice and darkness which imprison them. The snow melts, and the tundra springs alive with wild flowers and nesting birds — and the mosquitoes which buzz and bite anew each season. Old Sol, which most of the year is nonexistent, can pour its warmth earthward twenty-four hours a day. The men seem to come alive at this season, too, with bursts of apparently endless energy.

Medical research has found that the cold and dark of the Arctic winters slow up a man's efficiency to a marked degree. He walks more slowly, and it takes more energy to accomplish even a simple chore. To help counteract the effects of the elements, the men are fed 3000 to 4000 calories per day, and an abundance of high-protein foods and high-powered vitamins.

DEW Line employees live in the Arctic for eighteen months at a time, usually covering three to five stations during one tour of duty. If they're hired Outside — and most technical personnel are hired through the Federal Electric office in Paramus, New Jersey — they get their transportation paid up and back. If they decide to rehire after they've been out on vacation, their transportation is paid round-trip again.

Most DEW Line personnel say the eighteen months go fast. Many of the men are taking correspondence courses from leading universities to get their degrees in electrical engineering, or to upgrade themselves for better jobs on the DEW Line. Others are taking liberal arts courses, and one man is learning how to build yachts by mail.

For a job with all the disadvantages in the world, why do men sign up to work on the DEW Line?

The pay is good — very good. And that means take-home, or send-home pay. Board and room goes with the job.

The adventure of the high Arctic appeals to many. And others feel that the top of the continent is a good place to "get away from it all."

Technicians and scientists sign up because of the importance of the job and the challenge it affords. These scientists are dedicated men. They're accustomed to having their tasks take them to the remote ends of civilization.

As one electronics expert explained, "We're traveling through the electronics age with the speed of light. This means constant development in operating procedure and equipment. It's a tremendous challenge to work on the DEW Line."

How much is the DEW Line worth to the 49th state? As things stand today, this electronic shield in the Arctic represents about $12,000,000 annually, including wages and salaries of DEW Line employees.

The DEW Line is being stretched out farther and farther westward, and stations are now being constructed along the length of the Aleutians. More installations mean more employment, more purchasing of Alaskan goods and services. No longer does the Navy provide the flotilla for the annual Arctic resupply missions. It is contracted out, on bid, to a civilian barge line.

Two additional multi-million-dollar industries, interrelated with the DEW Line, are also proving of financial value to Alaska.

AC & W (Aircraft Control and Warning) is a *military* operation, not unlike the DEW Line, with wind-swept sites located along the *western* face of the new state, and a backfield of stations through Central and Southcentral Alaska. Like the DEW Line, AC & W is a vital factor in the geo-economic picture of the 49th state.

Backing up the AC & W is "White Alice," Alaska's newest communication system. Built for the defense of our nation, this system has brought, for the first time, communication with the outside world into many of Alaska's isolated civilian communities.

White Alice beams ultra-high frequency radio for distances of over two hundred miles at a single stride by bouncing part of its beam off the troposphere. It can carry many voices and telegraphic communication at the same time, and has conquered not only Alaska's lonely distances, but also the atmospheric fadeouts and static bombardments which have been so devastating a part of communication in the northern latitudes.

White Alice is a civilian operation. Its personnel are hired in Alaska, most of their families live in Alaska, own their homes here, and make up a high-quality segment of our citizenry.

What the future holds for the electronic defense of our continent is any man's guess. Super-radar, extending its effectiveness hundreds of miles beyond the present range, seems to be in immediate prospect.

Of this we may be sure: As long as the Communist political philosophy perils the Free World, as long as the Soviet Union is determined to use the threat of force against the West, the DEW Line, or its successor, will be our first line of defense.

16

Alaska's Number One Young Businessman

In 1940 A YOUNG MAN WAS DENIED A VISA TO Australia at the British Consulate in Los Angeles because he did not have a round-trip ticket or any visible means of support.

Today that young man's name is magic in the state of Alaska, and he has the golden touch. He has a most uncanny ability to see into the future, and this ability has already made him one of Alaska's wealthiest young citizens.

Walter Joseph Hickel, thirty-nine, is the personification of the old American adage, "Where there's a will, there's an Horatio Alger." Hailing from the village of Claflin, Kansas, the oldest son of ten children, Wally learned early in life to be self-reliant. His father, a German tenant farmer, taught his sons to think and act for themselves. His parents also gave him a good religious background.

When he was twenty, young Hickel traveled west to Los Angeles, planning to see the world. After he was turned down at the British Consulate, Hickel walked into a Los Angeles travel agency and asked, "Where can I go without a passport and a bunch of visas?"

"Alaska."

"Okay. How much is a one-way ticket? Steerage, I mean."

So Hickel bought a steerage ticket for $40 on the S.S. *Yukon* which sailed from Seattle in October, 1940. He arrived in Anchorage with 37 cents in his pocket.

That was the beginning of the odyssey of a young man with an infectious smile, boundless energy and a devastating personality. He is a vital force in Alaska, the father of five sons, a director in five corporations, and he can write a check for a million dollars.

Hickel's philosophy has always been, "If you make up your mind to do something, and you really want to do it, nothing will stop you." He applied this philosophy when jobs were hard to come by during his first month in Anchorage. He washed dishes for his meals. He cut brush for a pole line. He fired a boiler at the Alaska Railroad repair shops.

"Two Anchorage businessmen wanted to pep up the Fur Rendezvous in February, 1941, and offered a hundred and twenty-five dollars to anyone who would enter the ring with Jimmy Bayes, local pro boxer," Hickel explained. "A hundred and twenty-five dollars was a mountain of money to me then. I had never boxed professionally, but I needed that purse. I trained hard — and I beat him. I really gave him a whipping."

That started Hickel on his way. He held down two jobs for several years, bought an old house and carpentered it into a fine residence. He sold it at a handsome profit and quit working for wages. "I decided that the saw and hammer would be my coat of arms. I'd help build Alaska physically, if necessary."

In partnership with an old-timer he built four duplexes in Anchorage. They parlayed these into forty housing units. Then Hickel built forty units on his own. His next project was ninety-six living units. But he was looking far into the future.

Hickel believed that the newly constructed Alaska Highway would open new fields of opportunity in the tourist industry. He foresaw the day when the American traveling public would be pouring into the Land of the Midnight Sun as consistently as they are pouring into Arizona, Maine, Colorado and Canada. He believed that the de luxe motel, which has been such a success on the main highways of the States, would have an equally good future in Alaska.

He discussed his proposed half-million-dollar Traveler's Inn in Anchorage with bankers. They turned him down cold.

"I knew I was right, so I went ahead and bought the land and had the motel more than half completed before I got the financing arranged," Hickel stated with his usual enthusiasm.

The Traveler's Inn in Anchorage was immediately Alaska's sensational success in the hotel business. The bankers who had refused to finance him were the first to congratulate him and to admit their error.

Two years after the Traveler's Inn of Anchorage opened, Fairbanks citizens asked Hickel to duplicate his efforts in their city. Hickel did — on a larger and more de luxe scale. The Fairbanks Traveler's Inn added up to a cool million dollars when it opened in 1955. Beautifully decorated, with a restaurant featuring African lobster tail and Arctic sheefish, this motel is a showplace of Alaska.

As Hickel's business grew, he began to run up against the determined opposition of certain Stateside interests which had controlled Alaska's economic life and her politics since the Klondike days. He was aghast at the lengths they would go to stymie his projects. They wanted no rising young power in Alaska to bring competition to their control.

Hickel felt that it was morally wrong for a tight little group of businessmen outside Alaska to manipulate, for their own financial gain, the lives and destinies of the people of the Territory, and he made up his mind he would get into the fight. He could see that Alaska could never amount to much until it got political emancipation from these vested interests — until statehood were achieved.

Although Hickel says little about it, he has a deep religious conviction which provides the strength he needs when things go rough. He has a sense of honesty toward his fellow man that is refreshing to see. Principle, and a man's word, are basic tenets with Wally. It was the moral as well as the economic issue which first interested him in the political misfortunes of Alaska.

Hickel attended the 1952 GOP National Convention in Chicago as a private citizen. He astonished many delegates when he told them that the GOP in Alaska was a captive machine, that Alaskan politics were controlled in the States.

In 1953 the liberals in the Alaska legislature pushed through a law permitting both political parties to elect their national committeemen rather than have them appointed through machine politics. At the behest of liberal Alaskan Republicans, Hickel ran for Republican National Committeeman.

Despite violent opposition by vested interests, Hickel was elected by almost 2 to 1. But his victory was hollow. Upon advice of the Old Guard, the Republican National Committee refused to recognize the Alaskan election.

Hickel was refused admittance as a delegate to the National GOP meet in Cincinnati in 1954. He demanded a hearing, but it was apparent that the meeting would adjourn without listening to Hickel's case. Through pressure by his friends, a coalition of Western delegates, Hickel was finally voted in and seated just a few hours before the meeting adjourned.

But again he scored a hollow victory. The Outside interests which had controlled Alaskan politics for decades still did their work thoroughly in Washington circles. They wanted no committeeman from Alaska whom they could not control. As a result, Wally was not consulted when appointments affecting the Territory were being made, or when policy for the Northland was being formulated.

Hickel rolled up his sleeves. Defiantly he said, "Alaska demands freedom from political slavery. We demand an end to colonialism. Statehood is the answer — and the Republicans had better get with it if the party wants to stay alive in Alaska."

In 1955 Wally went to Washington with a planeload of Alaskans to push for statehood. He talked with every Republican official he could see. He laid Alaska's GOP grievances on the line. On his way back to Alaska he made a wide sweep through the States talking with national committeemen on the ills of the Republican party in Alaska and the urgency for statehood.

Hickel's political stature grew — both in the Territory where he was overwhelmingly re-elected as Republican National Committeeman, and in the States, where he was considered a growing power in GOP circles and a man to watch.

He spent more and more time on the fight for statehood. He was on the phone to Washington constantly, and, whenever the occasion demanded direct action, he called a dozen national committeemen in as many states to help him get a decision. His long distance bill was never less than a thousand dollars a month just on Alaskan affairs — and it came out of his own pocket.

When the drive for statehood rose to a climax in the nation's capital in June of 1958, Hickel was there as a member of the Republican team. With Secretary of the Interior Fred A. Seaton he marched up and down the halls of the Senate Office Building calling on Republican senators. Hickel's enthusiasm and his tremendous sales pitch on statehood helped win converts.

When the Senate finally voted to make Alaska the 49th state, Hickel mopped tears from his cheeks as did all of the Alaskan delegation. That evening Hickel made a statement he has repeated many times since, "Never — in all time — will Alaska ever have a greater economic impact than statehood."

The next day Hickel hastened homeward to go to work. Where business is concerned, this young man has a built-in crystal ball. Months before statehood became a reality, he had drafted his own plans for the future. He bought real estate in strategic locations throughout Alaska. He bought and optioned blocks of downtown Anchorage property. He announced a multimillion-dollar shopping center for the heart of an Anchorage suburb.

"Alaska can't help but grow by leaps and bounds with statehood," he contended. "We will need everything in large quantities, and we had better get ready now for the invasion of settlers."

In 1957 Hickel built thirty Anchorage residences in the $35,000 to $40,000 class and sold them before they were completed. In 1958 he built thirty more and sold them all. In 1959 he had thirty more under construction. Wally also found time to design and build a home for himself and his family — a $150,000 modern residence, beautifully decorated.

As Wally predicted, statehood started the investment ball rolling. Almost as soon as the Senate vote was in, Texas interests started coming north to talk with Hickel. New York banks and ultra-conservative Manhattan investment houses sent pin-striped vice-presidents to discuss Alaskan development.

It wasn't long before capital started coming in. Ground has been broken in Anchorage for branches of a nationally known grocery and a five-and-dime chain, and other chain stores are expected to follow suit shortly.

Hickel himself has announced plans for a $10,000,000 twelve-story office building and a twelve-story hotel, to be built in Anchorage on a spectacular site overlooking scenic Cook Inlet and Mt. McKinley. Both the Hickel Building and the Captain Cook Hotel are slated for the construction seasons of 1960 and 1961.

"The Captain Cook Hotel will do credit to any city of half a million people," Hickel stated with complete assurance, as if it were already an accomplished fact. "Relatively speaking, there will be nothing like it on the American continent.

"There is just one thing that worries me about this project," Hickel continued. "Before we can start construction, we're going to have to move two old apple trees that bloom so beautifully each spring. I'm just afraid they won't survive the change."

Hickel believes that Alaska will double in population in the next ten years. That will make it a state of almost half a million people. Then it will double again in the next ten. "Do you realize how many families that will be?" Wally exclaimed. "How many employed persons? How many homes — and how many babies?

"American capital now has a new field for investment. The American people have their first opportunity in a generation to satisfy their land hunger. Get these families and venture capital up here and Alaska will literally develop right up out of the ground," is Hickel's philosophy.

Hickel is more than a visionary, a lucky young man and an idealist who sees far into the future. He is a very shrewd businessman.

Wally has a large globe in his office, and he turned it slowly to show how closely Alaska's economic future is tied to the top third of the world. "The shortest route from the population centers of Europe to Asia and the Orient is over the north polar route," he explained. "From a practical standpoint, the halfway station on this route is Anchorage.

"Before the 49th state is much older, nine international airlines traveling between Europe and the Far East via the north polar region will be making scheduled stops at Anchorage. Each line will make from two to fourteen calls per week. Every plane arriving here will drop off from five to eight crew members who will have a layover or rest period of three to five days in the community. And as soon as the State Department and the CAB have worked out procedures, each international plane will be able to deposit in Anchorage from five to fifty layover passengers.

"Do you realize how important these passengers can be?" Wally exclaimed. "Hawaii catered to 142,000 layover passengers last year. That is 11,000 more than the number of tourists who went only as far as the mid-Pacific paradise to vacation. These layover passengers were guests of Hawaii for from one day to a month — and all that business was extra cash to the Islands.

"Here is the way I see Anchorage in the long-range global picture," Wally said seriously. He went on to point out that one of the subtle elements in hedging American investments in the world today is to sell the American philosophy of democracy, the American economy of abundance and high living standards.

"Anchorage, Alaska, will be the only contact for thousands of Europeans and Asians with the United States and with our American way of life," he continued. "We must treat them as honored guests. We must provide facilities which, during their brief stop or their layover, will do a bona fide selling job on America and our western ideals.

"The north polar flying business can be the catalyst that will make Anchorage an international city — if we get busy now and prepare for it. If we cannot accommodate the crews and passengers when they arrive — then the business will pass Alaska by. I, for one, do not intend to drag my feet on this now-or-never opportunity."

Wally seldom drags his feet on any opportunity. He has been in on Alaska's oil development almost since the first filings, and has high hopes that Alaska's production may surpass that of Texas.

"How fast the industry develops in Alaska depends on how fast the oil companies — and principally the independents — come in, put down wells and locate new fields," he said.

Another factor which will influence the speed of development of petroleum in Alaska, according to Hickel, is how fast our relations in the Middle East and elsewhere deteriorate. If our Middle East oil supply is cut off, we'll have to get oil somewhere else in a hurry. And if we should have trouble with Russia, we'll have to produce a sustaining supply of jet fuel, gasoline and other petroleum products in Alaska to take care of our first line of defense.

"Oil can mean to Alaska's economy what it means to Canada's," Hickel stated. "Have you been in Calgary and Edmonton lately? Their growths are examples of what can happen here."

How far can Hickel see into the future? Perhaps the best index to that ability is how far his judgment is trusted by the hard money that is now coming to Alaska for investment. Hickel is planning fifty years ahead, and capital is not at all reluctant to take his advice.

Within the next ten years, close to $30,000,000 will be invested in the state of Alaska by the Hickel investment companies. Investments in which Hickel will have a direct and personal interest will be much more than that.

"Before my time is up I expect to see a billion dollars of new American capital profitably invested in the new state, a million people living here, and Anchorage truly a northern window looking out on the world," said Alaska's number one young businessman.

Book Four

17

Vote "Yes" 3 Times

COLONEL M. R. "MUKTUK" MARSTON WAS MAK-
ing the rounds of the Kuskokwim Eskimo villages armed
with a persuasive tongue, an infectious smile, and a stack of
posters that said "VOTE 'YES' 3 TIMES."

Marston, a large, craggy man with a French beret and an
Eskimo parka, had been a familiar figure to the natives since
he helped organize and train the Alaska Territorial Guard
in World War II. When he talked they listened. They believed him, for he was their friend.

He assured the cautious villagers that statehood would
not take away their schools and confine them to reservations
as they had been told. He also explained that *each* of the
three statehood propositions would have to be marked
"Yes" or Alaska would not become a state.

After one particularly lengthy powwow, Muktuk turned
to a village leader and asked, "Now do you understand what
you do about voting?"

With a big grin the Eskimo recited. "We go to polls and
vote. Then we go home. We go to polls and vote again. Then
we go home. We go to polls and vote again. Then we go
home. Then we through voting."

Marston put back his head and roared. Unfortunately, he explained, you couldn't vote three times that way. You would have to mark all three ballots at one time.

That the natives believed the gospel according to Muktuk was evident at the ballot boxes. Native villages went overwhelmingly for statehood.

Whites and natives alike turned out en masse for this historic election. Voters included nineteen- and twenty-year-olds who were given the franchise under Alaska's new constitution.

For the first time in history Alaskans were being given the opportunity to decide their own destiny. They were voting for the right to run their own domain and make their own mistakes. When the ballots were counted, it was obvious that Alaskans wanted no more government by federal bureaus five thousand miles away. It was 5 to 1 for statehood!

That "Yes" vote on August 26, 1958, was the heartfelt culmination of a long, long crusade. Since the first Alaskan statehood bill was introduced into Congress in 1916, Alaskans old and new had fought for self-government as it was practiced in the 48 states. As Americans they wanted the right to vote for President. They wanted equal voting status in Congress. They wanted representation with their taxation. They wanted to be *first-class* American citizens.

Alaska served the longest apprenticeship of any would-be state in United States history. It was kept under wraps for ninety-two years principally by the large Outside interests who invested millions in the Territory and wanted no state government with its resultant taxing powers to interfere with their profits.

First the fur monopoly, then gold, fish and transportation interests set up their lobbies in Washington, D.C. When

Congress wanted information on Alaska it turned to these interests because they were the only sources available to give on-the-spot facts about the Northland.

The little man in Alaska was up against this organized lobby for so many years that the effort to gain representation and a measure of self-government became a great crusade to him. The residents of Sitka — the capital in early years — petitioned Congress for some type of self-government. But the lobbies said, "This isn't necessary. These people will be here today and gone tomorrow. If they make a few dollars they will leave Alaska. We are here to stay, and we know what's best for the Territory."

Over the years, despite the lobbies, the little man managed to acquire an Organic Act, a voteless delegate in Congress, and official territorial status. Then he started working for statehood.

As long as he agitated in his own backyard, the Outside interests kept hands off. They had their servants in both houses of the territorial legislature to see that no pinch was put on their pocketbooks.

But when the little man started shouting in the nation's capital, the lobbies cried "Foul!" After the Hon. James Wickersham of Alaska introduced the first statehood bill in the United States House of Representatives in 1916, salmon packers and gold interests shouted charges which echoed and re-echoed through the land for the next forty-two years:

"Alaska is not ready for statehood." "Alaska can't afford statehood." "Alaska's population is too small and too migratory." "Alaska doesn't have sufficient resources." "Alaska is too far away." "Alaska is not contiguous to the other states." "Alaska should be a state — but now is *not* the time."

To these arguments the Valdez *49th Star* retorted editorially: "Alaskans must either fight to make this a mighty northern state, or turn it over to the Seattle Arctic Club for a sheep pasture — the people of Alaska to be the lambs."

Through the years, whenever the anti-fisheries attitude grew too strong on the part of Alaskans, the canned salmon lobby used diversionary campaigns to "sectionalize" the Territory.

One of their tactics was the "partition plan." As far back as 1924 cannerymen prevailed upon some of the residents of Southeastern Alaska to send a spokesman to Washington to ask for statehood for the Panhandle only. Congressmen laughed him out of their offices. But thirty years later the same lobby dusted off the same plan and presented it as a last-ditch attempt to keep Alaska from its goal.

Alaska's fight for statehood ran into many blind alleys before it finally emerged from a maze of political frustration. Along the way it was guided, pushed, sidetracked and stymied by a number of government officials and Congressmen — in addition to the lobbyists.

Outstanding because of his aversion to Alaskans — and vice versa — was Secretary of the Interior Harold L. Ickes. His would-be reign over the northern Territory was so uncongenial that a strong statehood movement sprang up in the '30s to "rid Alaska of Czar Ickes!"

The "Old Curmudgeon" proposed huge European colonization schemes for Alaska, wanted reservations for natives, and forbade the issuance of any more homestead patents in the Territory. The crushing blow was his recommendation that all gold mines in Alaska be taxed a gross 8 per cent on production.

Alaska acquired an ally in her statehood fight with the appointment of a new governor, Dr. Ernest Gruening. Gruening, an aggressive foe of Ickes, was appointed by President Roosevelt in 1939 over the strongest objections of the Secretary of the Interior.

Gruening talked statehood at every opportunity — in Alaska, across the nation, and in the halls of Congress. He did much to catalyze Alaskan thinking and action toward the ultimate goal.

In his battle to advance the well-being of the Territory, Gruening clashed sharply with W. C. Arnold, the smart, affable general manager of the Alaska Canned Salmon Industry. For over twenty years, Bill Arnold — a handsome man in his fifties — was the strongest and most direct influence against Alaskan statehood.

Arnold did a magnificent job of convincing certain U.S. Senators and Representatives that the Territory was not ready to become a state.

He also paid a fee as a registered lobbyist at the territorial legislative sessions in Juneau. But his influence extended much farther than that. It was said that Bill Arnold "controlled" the territorial legislature, that he had "his men" in both houses to get favorable legislation for his clients. Bill has been spoken of as the "Boss of Alaska," and the "Most Powerful Man in the Territory."

During his more than thirteen years as governor, Gruening fought Arnold every inch of the way. He made statehood for Alaska his crusade.

Pushing the statehood cause in the United States Congress were Alaska's capable Delegate Anthony J. Dimond (1933-1945) and his popular and hard-working successor, E. L. "Bob" Bartlett (1945-1959). Members of both houses said it was a credit to the men Alaska sent to Washington that any legislation was passed that was favorable to the Northland. They had to get it by persuasion and friendship — they had no votes to trade.

As the statehood movement grew, Bartlett played an increasingly important role in winning Senators and Representatives. A sincere and convincing legislator, with the capacity for making and keeping many friends, he laid much of the groundwork for eventual Alaskan statehood.

Throughout the Territory, Alaskans lit the statehood torch and kept it burning. A 1946 Territory-wide referendum showed the nation that Alaskans were 3 to 2 in favor of becoming a state. This pro-statehood sentiment was largely inspired by the work of the newly formed Alaska Statehood Association, created by Evangeline Atwood of Anchorage. An able administrator, and wife of Robert B. Atwood, publisher of the pro-statehood *Anchorage Daily Times,* Mrs. Atwood saw to it that Alaskans old and new were acquainted with the arguments in favor of the statehood cause.

The territorial legislature, three years later, created an official Alaska Statehood Committee to fight for equal rights for Alaska. Publisher Atwood, an outstanding liberal, was named chairman of the committee, and Mildred Hermann, Juneau attorney, was appointed secretary-treasurer. A veteran at testimony on the stand, Mrs. Hermann was a convincing proponent of statehood before many a congressional committee.

During the nine years of the Alaska Statehood Committee, statehood bills were introduced into every session of the United States Congress, and every bill called forth reams of testimony. Alaskans chartered planes and flew to Washington to testify. Senators and Representatives flew to Alaska to hold hearings. Each new congressional group had to hear the story over again.

The most memorable junket was headed by anti-statehood Senator Hugh Butler of Nebraska, chairman of the powerful Interior and Insular Affairs Committee, who came to Alaska ostensibly so the "little man" could be heard.

The testimony the Senator heard from the "little man" was overwhelmingly for statehood. To dramatize their feeling, Anchorage citizens organized a "Little Men for Statehood" organization, and plastered the town with "I'm a Little Man for Statehood" signs and banners.

But Butler had arrived in Alaska adamantly opposed to statehood. He left in the same frame of mind.

Harry S. Truman became the first President to advocate statehood for Alaska and Hawaii in his State of the Union messages, and scores of important national organizations and individuals began to publicly endorse statehood for the Territory. In 1950 the Gallup Poll showed that the American public was 81 per cent in favor of statehood for Alaska.

Although both national party platforms endorsed statehood for Alaska, President Eisenhower, in his message to Congress in 1953, failed to mention statehood for the northern Territory. Eisenhower's allergy toward Alaska was partially responsible for keeping the Northland a territory for five years longer.

Despite the cool White House attitude, Bill Arnold and other lobbyists began to see the handwriting on the wall. Their best bet was to put off the fatal day as long as possible, so they adopted delaying tactics.

It was proposed that Alaska and Hawaii be given commonwealth status like Puerto Rico. This strategy crashed on takeoff, but it was a delaying measure. The 1924 joker of partition was again advocated by anti-statehood proponents.

To Alaskans it was not surprising that this partition plan

left *outside* of the state most of Alaska's best salmon fishing areas. The "Little Men" organization became "Operation Statehood," and crusading Alaskans flew to Washington to kill the partition plan.

With the recommendation and blessing of the Alaska Statehood Committee, Alaska's 1955 territorial legislature took matters into its own hands. It appropriated funds for a constitutional convention so that Alaska would be ready to step into the family of states.

Without waiting for authorization from Congress, Alaskans elected fifty-five delegates on a nonpartisan basis and sent them to the University of Alaska to write a constitution for the new state.

Alaska's constitution, which was completed in seventy-five days — the same length of time it took to write the Constitution of the United States — has been called "an ideal constitution" — "the best constitution ever written" — "a model for other states to follow."

Appended to the constitution, for approval by the voters, was the Alaska-Tennessee Plan, proposed by a New Orleans businessman by the name of George Lehleitner. Dubbed by convention delegates as "one of America's few moralists," Mr. Lehleitner played an important part in Alaska's admission into the Union.

He became interested in statehood for both Alaska and Hawaii while he served in the mid-Pacific with the Navy during the war, and did infinite research on the statehood question. Somewhere in America's political history he unearthed what was called the "Tennessee Plan," and made several trips to Alaska at his own expense to tell Alaskans and convention delegates how this plan could help Alaska get statehood.

This strategy, he explained, was used first by the Territory of Tennessee, and later by six other territories, to hasten their admission into the Union. They elected two "Senators" and one "Representative" *in advance* of becoming a state and sent them to Washington to lobby for statehood.

When the voters balloted to accept Alaska's new constitution, they also approved George Lehleitner's Alaska-Tennessee Plan. Alaskans elected former Governor Ernest Gruening and constitutional convention president William Egan as "Senators," and former Alaskan attorney general Ralph Rivers as "Representative" to push the statehood cause in the nation's capital.

These unofficial legislators opened offices in Washington, D.C., and, with Alaska's voteless delegate, Bob Bartlett, proceeded to sell members of both houses on statehood for Alaska.

In 1957-1958, eleven statehood bills were introduced in the 85th Congress. For ten months the final bill was bottled up in the powerful House Rules Committee, dominated by a Southern Democrat-Republican coalition which was not about to allow a liberal Territory like Alaska to join the Union.

Finally, Democratic Congressmen Wayne Aspinall (Colo.) and Leo O'Brien (N.Y.) of the House Interior Committee invoked an ancient rule under which statehood legislation is privileged legislation, and can be brought to the floor without action of the Rules Committee. Speaker Sam Rayburn upheld them.

Opponents soon found that they could not defeat the bill. But they could amend — and, urged by the lobbies, amend they did. They saw to it that the federal government retained control of Alaska's fisheries, and added three propositions to the bill which would have to be approved by Alaskans. If they voted down even one of the propositions, Alaskans would not get statehood.

These propositions (1) called for yet another Alaskan referendum on statehood; (2) stated, in a confusingly worded paragraph, that the boundaries of the state would be the same as the boundaries of the Territory; and (3) stated, in ambiguous legalese, that Alaska would accept the conditions under which federal grants of land were made to the state.

With these amendments, the Alaska statehood bill passed the House on May 28, 1958, by a vote of 208 to 166.

Statehood proponents now marshaled all their forces for the big push in the Senate. The lobbyists deployed their friends, and brought forth all the time-worn arguments, along with a few choice new ones: the House bill was a poor bill and not in the best interests of the Territory; Alaska was overwhelmingly Democratic — it would automatically elect Democratic legislators.

Here Secretary of the Interior Fred Seaton displayed his generalship. Republican Seaton had been one of Alaska's strongest boosters, and had finally brought President Eisenhower around to endorsing statehood for Alaska.

Seaton called prominent Alaskan Republicans back to the nation's capital to convince Republican lawmakers that Alaska should have statehood. They worked day and night talking and convincing.

The Alaska statehood bill consumed six days of debate in the Senate. Southern Senators tried every trick to scuttle or sidetrack the bill. But the proponents let the opposition talk itself to a whisper.

On June 30, after a session that extended into the evening, all opposition collapsed. The threatened Southern filibuster evaporated. Shortly before 8 P.M. the Senate voted 64 to 20 in favor of making Alaska the 49th state!

The news flashed in at 4 P.M. Juneau time, 3 P.M. Skagway time, 2 P.M. Anchorage time, and 1 P.M. Nome time. Alaskans, who had been glued to their radios since early morning, were stunned at the suddenness of the vote. Many wept unashamedly. And all — each in his own way — offered thanks for this historical moment. It was a day of thanksgiving rather than a day of celebration.

What caused the 85th Congress to grant statehood to Alaska, when all previous Congresses had failed? The vote didn't just happen. Through the years, by hard work of many Alaskans and dedicated Stateside citizens, the cause for statehood had been building up in the minds of the American people.

The American feeling for the underdog who deserves better treatment is a powerful influence on our body politic. Thousands of Americans from all the states wrote letters to their Senators and Representatives urging them to vote for statehood for Alaska. This was a potent force from constituents to which elected officials gave proper attention.

The press of the nation put on a drive the like of which Congress had not seen in years. Public media pulled out all stops and added to the crescendo.

Let no one think it was any single trick or "gimmick" that finally put Alaskan statehood over the goal line. It was team work of the highest order, and a bipartisan effort of both political parties.

It was a combination of all these factors, and others, which finally wrote a successful "finis" to Alaska's statehood chapter. As one legislator said, "Statehood could no longer be denied. It was Alaska's time in history!"

On July 7, President Eisenhower signed the statehood bill. From then on, the rest was up to Alaskans. They would have to show they wanted statehood by voting for the three propositions.

The lobbies transferred their scene of battle to Alaska to try to defeat the statehood election. They threw everything they had into the fight, and rumors flew that federal employees would lose their jobs, that one of the propositions would take away precious rights of Alaskans, that natives would have to live on reservations.

The Alaska Statehood Committee, Operation Statehood, many other organizations and hundreds of individuals got into the fray and urged their countrymen to "Vote 'Yes' 3 Times." They did.

This time the little man was in the driver's seat. The lobbies were out and Alaska was in!

From then on, only the formalities remained. Alaskans elected their "voting" representation in the United States Congress: Senators Ernest Gruening and Bob Bartlett, and Representative Ralph Rivers. They also voted for their first elective Governor — William Egan.

President Eisenhower officially proclaimed Alaska the 49th state on January 3, 1959. On July 4 of this same year Americans officially flew their new 49-star flag — the first change in design since 1912.

How great a part Alaska plays in the family of states remains to be seen. Alaskans are sure that their new state will be an outstanding social, economic and political addition to the U. S. A.

18

The Crystal Ball

Everyone wants a look into Alaska's future.
What is the Northland going to be like ten, twenty, thirty
years from now? How fast will Alaska grow into a big state
— big in population, big in industry and big in productive
wealth?

The answers to these questions lie, in large part, with
Uncle Sam.

American history shows that the federal government has
been the major force in developing our great nation as it expanded westward. Since 1806, when Congress appropriated
$30,000 for a wagon road over the Alleghenies so that people
could settle in the wilderness of the West, the United States
has invested large sums in building roads to let new lands
be homesteaded. It has invested large sums in power and
irrigation projects so that the new land could be more productive and support more people.

This has been the history of the West. And Uncle Sam's
investment has paid off handsomely.

Today Alaska stands on the same threshold of development as did the fledgling areas across the continent in the
nineteenth century.

Based on what has gone before, it is entirely logical

to predict that Uncle Sam will treat the 49th state with the same consideration and interest as he has treated the other members of his large family.

Even though Alaska was a late arrival in the family — forty-seven years after New Mexico and Arizona — with a generous amount of federal help it shouldn't be long before No. 49 will equal many of the other states in population and wealth.

Ben Crawford, youthful president of the City National Bank of Anchorage, stated that "Alaska is going to get population whether it gets anything else or not. But the two catalysts which will spark the growth and development of the Northland are roads and power. These two catalysts will help us solve many of the problems of big-scale progress up here.

"Other bankers share our views," he went on. "The Twelfth District Federal Reserve Bank of San Francisco made a study of Alaska and here is what one of its bulletins says about the development of the new state:

" 'If the Federal government finds it possible in the course of the next decade or two to earmark considerable amounts for Alaskan development, to be allocated mainly to providing transportation, power, aids to agriculture, and loans to business, more of Alaska may be transformed into a desirable place for human habitation, adding pleasure, depth, and variety to the culture of the nation.' "

When Alaska became a state, it had a bare five thousand miles of roads, about half of them blacktopped. But no Alaskan road would qualify as better than a "secondary paved road" in the Lower 48. Imagine a state over twice the size of Texas with but five thousand miles of road. The Lone Star state has 196,000 miles.

When the Federal Highway Act was passed by Congress in 1916, Alaska, having no voting representation in the nation's capital, was specifically excluded. The same influences which stymied Alaska's development for decades convinced Congress that Alaska's share would be better spent in the other states. Figures released recently by the Bureau of Public Roads establish that, had Alaska been included in the Federal Highway Act, it would have received not less than $300,000,000 and as high as $575,000,000 for road construction. And a splendid trans-Alaskan highway system would exist today.

The need for an immediate lump-sum highway appropriation is urgent. If a road-building program does not get started without delay, cars and families will be backed up for miles in their quest for land on which to homestead.

As we write this chapter, there are families camped on the bank of the Susitna River at Talkeetna, 112 miles north of Anchorage, waiting for flood waters to subside so they can row across the river and fan out into the wilderness to pick out homesteads in the wide, fertile, roadless Susitna Basin. The need for roads in other areas is just as dramatic and urgent.

A comprehensive statewide transportation system, to show Congress where millions of acres of Alaskan land can be opened to exploration, development and settlement, has been blueprinted by Alaska's Senator Ernest Gruening. Included in this overall transportation picture is a much-needed ferry system to release the towns of Southeastern Alaska from their isolation and to connect them with the rest of the state, give them access to the Alaska Highway and to the British Columbia highway system at Prince Rupert.

Even if Congress does provide funds this session, it will

take time to get a large-scale road-building program under way in Alaska. An unbelievable amount of fieldwork, engineering and drafting must be done, camps must be established in the wilderness, and two or three years could elapse before giant bulldozers and carryalls bite into the soil of Alaska on an extensive trans-state highway system. In the Big Part of Alaska, climate holds the road-building season down to six months a year.

Concurrent with a mighty road program for Alaska is the need for hydro-power development. If Alaska is to grow into a vital national supply house of productive wealth, it must have an abundance of cheap power.

Alaska has been power-hungry for years. Until recently, a good many Alaskans were paying as high as 15 cents per kilowatt for electricity. Not too many years ago, Anchorage housewives cooked their dinners in shifts because there wasn't enough electricity and sections of the residential areas were cut off during certain hours. The downtown business district had brown-outs, and the power shortage spread to the Matanuska Valley before the 30,000-kw Bureau of Reclamation hydroelectric plant at Eklutna was completed.

Right now, it is nip and tuck as to whether the new 15,000-kw Cooper Lake REA-sponsored project can get into operation before electricity again becomes critical in the Anchorage area.

The Federal Power Commission reports that Alaska must double her power output in the next ten years, and then double it again, just to keep up with the normal growth of the Northland. This does not take into consideration the development of new large industries in the state.

The U.S. Corps of Engineers declares that the state of Alaska has two hundred power sites which can economically produce two thirds as much electricity as is now generated in all of the forty-eight continental states combined.

There is one power site on the list that staggers the imagination. This is the proposed Rampart Dam on the Yukon River, which would be the largest power generator in the world — even exceeding anything planned in the USSR.

This power colossus would be almost twice the size and capacity of Grand Coulee Dam. The Rampart reservoir would be larger than Lake Erie, take fifteen years to fill, and would back water up 300 miles to the Canadian border.

A power source of that size could establish Alaska as an industrial giant, and its possibilities are beyond our present perspective.

An industrialist in a worldwide corporation told the members of the Alaska Development Board, "If a great supply of cheap power were to be developed at the North Pole, industry would find a way to pipe it out, or devise a method of getting raw materials to it." He pointed out that raw materials are now brought from the ends of the earth to ports where an abundance of cheap power makes processing economical and profitable.

Alaska can be in this category in a few years, if the Rampart Dam is built and a transmission grid is strung to the seaports of the new state.

The necessity for immediate hydroelectric power construction has been urged by Alaska's Senior Senator Bob Bartlett. He stated that a start at low-cost power development must be made without delay, "so we can wire Alaska for an orderly and rapid growth."

"This rapid growth of Alaska may be virtually an explosion," Elmer E. Rasmuson, president of the National Bank of Alaska, stated. "By the year 2000 there will be two billion

232   *Alaska, U.S.A.*

more people on earth, and the Arctic regions of the globe will
be called upon to supply food in vast quantities for these
new mouths. The unturned soil and undeveloped resources of
our Northland will provide homes and incomes for our expanding population much sooner than we realize.

"There are countless new phases to the future that we must
take into consideration," he continued. "I feel that many tech-
nological breakthroughs will occur which will be vital to the
new state. Just one of the possibilities may be the use of the
atom bomb, as proposed by Dr. William Teller, to create harbors along Alaska's coastline where none exist today. Like-
wise, the possible release of vast quantities of petroleum by
subsurface nuclear fission could be of major significance to
Alaska.

"Our biggest problem is to keep our sights high enough to
encompass the future developments which will cascade upon
us."

Even if power giants are built, and the necessary transmission grids bring cheap power to tidewater along Alaska's
coastline, the new state's pattern of industrial development
will differ greatly from that of the Lower 48.

"The traditional type of American industry, with forests
of smokestacks belching smog over the countryside, will not
exist in Alaska," said Robert B. Atwood, publisher of the
Anchorage *Daily Times*. "Those smokestacks are symbols of
nineteenth-century industry.

"For its industrial development, the new state will depend
on automation and the latest scientific discoveries — as well
as new enterprises and new processes yet to be invented.

"This is what I mean: right now more than fifty per cent of
the wage earners in Southcentral Alaska are employed in jobs
that did not exist fifteen years ago. Microwave communica-

tion is a major payroll here. Electronics already is high in our category of gainful occupations."

Outside risk capital and investment funds are coming to Alaska increasing amounts. With new perspective, they are redesigning old businesses as well as establishing new ones.

Coming in for its share of face-lifting is Alaska's fishing industry. Right here we'd like to trace a finger along Alaska's long, serrated coastline and say, "The waters of Alaska have produced a billion dollars in fish in the years gone by, and the potential has hardly been estimated."

Even though the annual runs of salmon are on the decline, and the present fishing outlook is not bright, Alaska's Commissioner of Fisheries, Clarence Anderson, believes that the runs of salmon will be rebuilt and whole new fields in fish can be developed. New investors in new phases of one of Alaska's oldest and most profitable industries stand to reap new fortunes from Alaska's waters.

A summary of the future of the fishing industry was made by the editors of the *Alaska Sportsman,* an excellent monthly magazine that puts Alaska's best foot forward.

"Our over-all opinion of the fish industry is that fish will, for many years to come, be Alaska's main dollar item — that within a few years strict conservation practices will bring salmon back to higher levels than today — the shellfish industry will continue to grow — and good home packs of various Alaska fish products should find an increasing direct-mail sales market if small packers are content to market only small volume and to maintain high quality."

Because of Alaska's geographical position, it has outstanding opportunities to create cultural and business relationships with other countries — both to the east and to the west.

Officially, Alaska's state government should establish a

commission to extend hands across the border to our Canadian neighbors. Every time we drive to the other states we are guests of Yukon Territory and British Columbia. If we are heading to the East Coast the short way we use the excellent thoroughfares of several other provinces.

British Columbia and Yukon Territory are interested in the development of the north country, and so is Alaska. We have mutual problems in pushing back the frontier. At present, upper British Columbia is experiencing a breathtaking boom in land settlement, oil development and industrial growth. Six hundred million dollars in Swedish capital is reported ready for hydroelectric construction there. We can learn much from Canada.

To the west, Alaska has an interested neighbor in the Japanese empire. Japan needs the timber, oil and coal of Alaska, and has already invested more than $50,000,000 in a pulp mill at Sitka. This plant ships its entire production of pulp to Japan.

If present plans mature, official Japanese funds will be heavily invested in oil and coal production in the 49th state. Alaska would be well advised to encourage friendship and financial and cultural ties with the Orient.

Alaska's commanding position on the globe will play an increasing role in the years ahead. Already one world-wide construction company has recognized that its Anchorage office is closer to many points in the Pacific than are its west coast offices.

Morrison-Knudsen Company has announced that its Anchorage office will be in charge of contracts on Okinawa, Formosa, the Philippines, Kwajalein, Guam and other points in the Pacific. It is simple economics — less mileage, less travel time. Key personnel in Alaska will work in warmer climates during the winter months when there isn't too much construction going on in the 49th state.

So far in this chapter we have outlined the major things that can happen *to* Alaska in the next ten, twenty or thirty years. Now let us reverse the direction of our thinking. What will Alaska contribute to the nation as a result of statehood?

George Lehleitner, shortly after the University of Alaska conferred on him an honorary degree for his contribution to statehood, discussed this question.

"Let us recall a constantly recurring sequence of events in world history that has not varied since the beginning of time," Lehleitner said.

"The emergence of a people onto the pages of history is a slow and labored process. They are united by long oppression. Slowly they gain strength and character. In bitter conflict they win their freedom. They reach out, subdue other tribes, till the soil, build cities and become a powerful nation. They rise to a peak in art, culture, government and authority in their world. They consolidate their boundaries and, for a time, live in a golden age. Then they rest on their laurels and are self-sufficient unto themselves. With that complacency a virus invades their fabric. History's inexorable end to this pattern is conquest and destruction.

"Only so long as a nation continues to grow, can that nation resist the dangers of decay.

"Now let us look at the United States, *without* rose-colored glasses," Lehleitner continued. "The size and shape of the United States was established over a hundred years ago. Unconsciously our political philosophy, our economic thinking, and our social outlook have become stylized by the boundaries of our great nation.

"If we be honest, we must admit that certain economic and

social ills within our nation are being treated with palliatives, not unlike the cake and grain given the Romans by the latter Caesars.

"Opponents of Alaskan statehood were completely sincere in declaring that the traditional 48 states were big enough for the American nation. But let us be thankful, for our children and our children's children, that the American people chose to include Alaska in the union.

"The admission of Alaska assures the American nation of continued growth for years and years to come," he said. "Alaska will be an outlet for our people, for our social energies, for our economic vitality and our mental capacities for decades.

"I no longer have fears for our country. Alaska will provide bountifully the opportunity for leadership, culture and human progress which only time can properly evaluate," George Lehleitner pointed out.

"In our lifetime we will see only the beginning of Alaska's true contribution to the American nation. But the next generation, and the next, will be the benefactors of the wisdom of having granted statehood to Alaska.

"America will continue to grow."

Index

Potato farming, 121-122, 144, 145-146, 147-149, 150
Poultry and egg industry, 120-121
Power development, 230-232
Pribilof Islands, 10
Prices, 58-60
Prince William Sound, 34
Prospectors, 182, 185-187
Providence Hospital, 35
Pulp mills, 27, 31, 234

RADAR DEFENSES. *See* DEW Line
Railroads, 15, 32, 33, 34-35. *See also* Alaska Railroad
Rainfall, 28. *See also* Weather data
Rampart Dam, 231
Rasmuson, Elmer R., 231
Rayburn, Sam, 223
Red Devil mine, 188
Red Dog Saloon, 30
Reeve Aleutian Airways, 128
Reindeer, 139
Religion, 56-57
Religious organizations, 57
Republican National Convention of 1952, 206
Resurrection Bay, 36, 37
Retail Clerks Union, 93
Richardson Highway, 34, 160
Richfield Oil Company, 177
Rick of High Ridge, 68
Rivers, Ralph, 223, 226
Roadhouses, 69, 162-163
Roads, 34, 40, 64-74, 228-230
Roosevelt, Franklin D., 16, 181
Royal Canadian Mounted Police, 73
Rural Electrification Administration, 104, 105, 146, 149
Russian-American Company, 7, 10
Russians, 5-7

ST. MICHAEL, CATHEDRAL OF, 31
St. Paul, ship, 5
St. Peter, ship, 5-6
Salaries, 59-60
Salmon, 14, 28, 37
Salvation Army, 57-58, 87

Saxman, 28
Schools, 31, 53-56
Schrock, Morris, 82-85, 88, 91, 92, 95, 97
Seaton, Fred A., 208, 224
Service clubs, 49
Seward, 36
Seward, William Henry, 8
Seward Peninsula, 13
Shaw, Robert, 61
Sheep farming, 126-130
Sheldon Jackson Junior College, 31
Shrimp, 37-38
Siberia, 27
Sitka, 8-9, 26, 30-31, 66, 217
Sitkalidak Island, 137
Skagway, 14, 31, 32, 66
Skookum Jim, 13
Smith, Soapy, 14, 32
Standard Oil of California, 77, 177
State of Alaska Department of Mines, 184
Statehood, struggle for, 8, 207-208, 216-226
Steel Creek Road, 145, 146
Stikine River, 29
Stimple, Bert, 141-152
Stimple, Leah ("Snukie"), 141, 144, 145, 147, 148, 149, 150, 151
Stines, Norman, 15-16
Stoeckl, Baron Edouard de, 8
Stores, 93, 209
Strandberg Brothers, 185
Streator, Illinois, 194
Sullivan, Ed, 61
"Summer Study Group," 193
Susitna Flats, 134
Susitna River, 229

TAGISH CHARLIE, 13
Talkeetna, 229
Tanana River, 13
Tanana Valley, 117, 134, 141, 146-147, 148, 151
Tanana Valley Farmers, 148
Teal, John J., Jr., 138
Telegraph Creek, 29